Light *for the* Journey

Light
for the
Journey

75 Devotional Reflections from Cross-Cultural Experiences

Rosella M. Kameo

© 2011 by Rosella Kameo. All rights reserved.

WinePress Publishing (PO Box 428, Enumclaw, WA 98022) functions only as book publisher. As such, the ultimate design, content, editorial accuracy, and views expressed or implied in this work are those of the author.

No part of this publication may be reproduced, stored in a retrieval system, or transmitted in any way by any means—electronic, mechanical, photocopy, recording, or otherwise—without the prior permission of the copyright holder, except as provided by USA copyright law.

All Scriptures quoted are from the *Holy Bible, Life Application Study Bible, New Living Translation*. 2nd Edition Copyright ©1996, 2004, 2007 by Tyndale House Foundation.

ISBN 13: 978-1-4141-2127-7
ISBN 10: 1-4141-2127-X
Library of Congress Catalog Card Number: 2011932000

For my husband, Daniel, and son, Peter,
with gratitude and love

Contents

Acknowledgments xi
Introduction xiii
Chapter 1: Faith and Trust 1
    The Stubborn Bulls 3
    The Road of Life 5
    In Whom Should We Trust? 8
    A Leap of Faith 10
    God's Provision 13
Chapter 2: God's Nature and Will 15
    Calling God Father 17
    Talking with God 20
    Father Knows Best 22
    God's Will 24
    The Silent Hand of God 26
    What's It Like? 28

Chapter 3: Our Identity 31
- Who Are You? 33
- What's in a Name?. 35
- My Dumb Daughter 37
- Being Yourself 39
- A Chosen People 41
- In His Image 43
- Duck Paws 46
- Dressing As a Christian 48

Chapter 4: Living in Grace 51
- The Flagellant 53
- Free Indeed! 55
- Just Tell Me What To Do! 57
- Earning God's Favor 59
- To Eat or Not To Eat 61

Chapter 5: Walking in the Light 63
- Dulled by Familiarity 65
- Waiting in Hope 68
- Joy in an Indian Village 71
- The Sacred and the Secular 74
- Feeling Foolish 77
- Strength Through Weakness 80
- Showing Discernment 82
- Living Witnesses 84
- In Spite of Us 86

Chapter 6: Confronting Adversity 89
- Are You There, God? 91
- Facing Loss 93
- The Test of Courage 95

When Disaster Strikes 97
When the Earth Shook 99
Modern Day Miracle 101
Hope for a New Day 104

Chapter 7: Facing Fear 107
Things That Go Bump in the Night 109
God's Peace 111
Calming the Storm Within Us 113
Panic in Jerusalem 115
A Living Nightmare 117

Chapter 8: Doing What's Right 119
The Importance of Integrity 121
Save the Children 123
Digging Out the Roots 125
A Knock at the Door 127
Of Dogs and Footwear 129
Wise Choices 131

Chapter 9: Giving and Receiving 133
Filling the Baskets 135
Corn and Beans 137
For Just Such a Time as This 140
Sharing Burdens 142
The Gift of Listening 144
A Perfect Stranger 146
By Our Love 148
One of Them 151
Across Cultural Divides 154
Let Me Help! 157

Chapter 10: A Matter of Perception............... 159
    Looking Beneath the Surface...................... 161
    Different Perspectives............................. 163
    Friendship Is the Best Policy 165
    But Aren't the Jews Christian?..................... 167
    Different Cultural Lenses.......................... 169
    We and They..................................... 171

Chapter 11: Promoting Harmony 173
    High Maintenance................................ 175
    Winning the Battle 177
    The Test of Tolerance............................. 179
    To Know Them Is To Love Them 181
    Ulterior Motives 184
    Breaking Down the Stereotypes.................... 186
    Bridging the Ravine.............................. 188
    Finding Common Ground......................... 192

Endnotes 195

Scriptural Index................................ 199

Acknowledgments

ALTHOUGH THIS BOOK is a reflection on my own cross-cultural experiences, I feel indebted to many individuals and organizations.

First, I am deeply grateful to the Evangelical Lutheran Church in America (ELCA) and its predecessor body, the Lutheran Church in America, for giving me the opportunity to serve the church overseas. Thank you to the staff of Global Mission for providing me with loving support every step of the way. I would particularly like to recognize Dr. J. F. Neudoerffer (1918-1995), who hired me as a young short-termer and served as my program director, mentor, and father for much of my overseas career. With vision, compassion, and good humor, "Uncle Fred" paved the way for many an adventure included in this book.

My sponsoring congregations in the ELCA deserve special mention as well. Whether during visits to your congregation or through letters, your thought-provoking questions helped me to serve with eyes wide open and to recognize how effective stories and anecdotes can be in getting the message across when cultural landscapes differ.

On a more personal level, I would like to thank Anne Fichthorn, soul mate and travel companion, for reading the first copy of the manuscript and offering so many insightful suggestions. Your friendship has been one of the greatest blessings of my life. I am also deeply grateful to Shirley Smith Franklin, a special sister in the faith. Thank you for encouraging me to write and offering so many valuable tips along the way. I am indebted as well to Dusty Knisely. Your own cross-cultural experiences, keen vision, faith, and uplifting spirit have shaped my thinking profoundly.

A very special tribute goes to my husband, Daniel. As my best friend and most trusted critic, you are the first reader of everything I write and the one who inspires me the most in all that I do. I would also like to thank my sister-in-law and close companion, Vera Kameo. With wit, grace, and charm, you have so willingly helped me to make sense of the many cultural experiences we have shared together within our Indonesian extended family and beyond.

Finally, this book could never have been written without the countless individuals, named and unnamed, who appear in these reflections—my former students, teaching colleagues, missionaries, local supervisors, hosts and friends, particularly those from India, Kashmir, Hong Kong, the Palestinian Territories, and Indonesia. Thank you for sharing the light and enlarging my vision. By helping me to see the world in new ways, you have broadened my horizons and enriched my life more than you will ever know. To God be the glory!

Introduction

AS A TWENTY-YEAR-OLD ready to begin my senior year in college, I flew to New York City for a job interview that would change the course of my life.

"What brings you to New York?" an airport cabbie asked as he drove me to our church headquarters on 42nd Street. When I told him I had come to apply for a job with the Lutherans to teach in India, he shook his head despondently. "You know, you're making a big mistake!" he exclaimed. "You ought to be making the most of your life while you're young, not heading off across the world to India."

I smile now when I recall that conversation. What could be more worthwhile, inspirational, and exciting than to serve the church overseas and experience other cultures, languages, and traditions? As I was sent on assignments to Asia and the Middle East, I began to see the world with different eyes. I learned to expect the unexpected and to appreciate the richness of life which had come to me by the grace of God. Marriage to an Indonesian brought a wealth of new cross-cultural experiences as well and a chance to deepen my understanding of our differences and similarities. The stories kept growing.

"You ought to write a book!" friends and supporting congregations would say as I eventually neared retirement. True, but what kind of a book? How could I meaningfully share my cross-cultural experiences with others in a useful way? It was then that I decided to write a book of meditations based on personal experiences. Arranged by theme, each would include a Bible verse, questions for reflection, and a prayer. *Light for the Journey* was born.

Whether you use this book individually or in a group, I hope that you too will be blessed by the cross-cultural experiences that have enriched my life. Now, if only I could share them with that cabbie!

—**Rosella M. Kameo**

Chapter 1

Faith and Trust

Faith is not belief without proof but trust without reservation.[1]

—Elton Trueblood

The Stubborn Bulls

―⚜―

The Lord says, "I will guide you along the best pathway for your life. I will advise you and watch over you. Do not be like a senseless horse or mule that needs a bit and bridle to keep it under control."
—Psalm 32:8-9

THE OLD MISSIONARY chuckled as she sat down beside me and began reminiscing over her lifelong career as a Bible Woman in Andhra Pradesh, South India.

"You know," she said, "I began my career right here where you are now, studying Telugu at Schade School in Rajahmundry. When I had become fluent enough, I was sent to work in Bhimavarum."

Pausing to wipe her glasses, she continued, "A funny thing happened

when it came time for me to move to Bhimavarum. All of my belongings were loaded onto a bullock cart for the overnight journey, and I climbed up into the back along with them. As the animals plodded along, I was lulled to sleep. The driver sitting in the front must have fallen asleep too."

"What happened then?" I asked.

"Well, the next morning when we woke up," she continued, "the bullock cart was standing still. There we were, right back here at Schade School where we had started out the day before! During the night, those Brahma bulls had taken matters into their own hands, turned around, and gone back home the way they had come."

As I laughed at her story, I thought of how often we must seem like those Brahma bulls to God. Submission does not come easy for most of us. We say we trust God. We ask God for guidance. Yet deep down we still think we know best and refuse to give up the controls.

When we insist on doing things our own way, though, are we being as useful to God as we should be? Are we leaving enough room for God to work through us? Like those Brahma bulls, even though we do not always know where our owner is taking us, we have to trust that He knows best.

For Reflection

1. Why do we so often forget to involve God in our planning and decision-making?
2. Why is it easier for most of us to set off on our own instead of following God's lead?
3. In what areas of life do you find it most difficult to turn your independence and self-reliance over to God's control?

Help us to recognize our need for you, oh Lord. Give us the courage to follow you even when we do not know where you are leading us.

The Road of Life

~~~

Seek his will in all you do, and he will show you which path to take.

—Proverbs 3:6

"HOW DO I get myself into these things?" I asked Ruth, my teaching colleague at Lutheran Middle School in Kowloon, Hong Kong, as we tried to keep up with the forty-eight Chinese students ahead of us. The school day had ended, and my ninth

graders, still wearing their white school uniforms, had prepared an after-school birthday surprise for me.

"Where on earth are they taking us?" I asked as we tromped through the lobby of the Kwong Wah Hospital and out the back door to Dundas Street. On we walked, up Fa Yeun Street, over to Tung Choi, and through a maze of lanes. My students were not lost, but I certainly was. My students knew exactly where we were going, but I didn't have a clue.

Suddenly, as we turned a corner, they opened a door and shouted, "We're here!"

Where? Why, McDonalds, of course! I was flabbergasted. To celebrate my birthday, they had arranged a kiddie party for the whole class, complete with hats, balloons, and noise-makers.

That's the way life is. Even though we have been promised an eventual heavenly feast, the future remains a mystery. Sometimes we don't know which path our lives will take and we struggle to make sense of it all. Will we wind up marrying the person we are dating? Will we be accepted at the college of our choice? Will we ever find another job if we leave the current one? Along the road of life so often we feel confused and uncertain.

Despite our confusion, though, there is no need to panic. We may not recognize which street we are on or just where we are headed at the moment, but we can certainly trust the hand that is leading us there.

For Reflection

1. What are you feeling confused about right now in your journey of life?
2. What are the attributes of trust? How can we acquire them?

3. How can we best help others who are feeling lost? Offer three suggestions.

When we cannot see what lies ahead, give us the faith to trust you and the courage to follow you, through Jesus Christ our Lord.

In Whom Should We Trust?

> Do not defile yourselves by turning to mediums or to those who consult the spirits of the dead. I am the Lord your God.
> —Leviticus 19:31

OUR NEIGHBOR WAS terribly worried about her married daughter. During the night the daughter's stomach had become distended and a lump had appeared at the back of her neck. Obviously, someone with evil intentions had used black magic to insert something inside of her body to harm her.

Our neighbor took her daughter to a trusted shaman who was able to consult with the spirits of the dead and perform black magic. He told her to bring her daughter to a remote spot out of town that night. When she went there to meet him, he withdrew a Javanese dagger from the daughter's stomach and a bundle of pins from the back of her neck. A few nights later, at the instruction of the shaman, our neighbor took the dagger to Yogyakarta's Parangtritis beach and hurled it into the sea. The shaman then magically inserted a precious stone into the daughter's stomach to protect her from any other object that might be sent to harm her.

Using a shaman isn't cheap. For "healing" our neighbor's daughter, the shaman had charged her ten times her monthly salary. We feel angry that our neighbor was victimized by her ignorance. We are also concerned because using mediums, shamans, or sorcerers is an unforgiveable sin in Islam, and our neighbor considers herself to be a good Muslim.

What should we do when we feel trapped by dangers or threats? In whom do we trust? To whom should we turn?

For Reflection

1. Have you ever been tempted to use a medium, shaman, sorcerer, or other source of power? What were the circumstances?
2. What is the harm in turning to mediums, psychics, clairvoyants, and soothsayers?
3. In what other ways do we show a lack of trust in the living God?

May we recognize you, the living God, as the only true source of power. Help us to trust totally in you and not to be tempted by what might defile us or harm our relationship with you.

A Leap of Faith

Faith is the confidence that what we hope for will actually happen; it gives us assurance about things we cannot see.
—Hebrews 11:1

Indonesia

HE WAS A simple, trusting man—a Christian farmer named Thobias from a remote village in West Timor in eastern Indonesia. He had a sixth-grade education, like everyone else in the village, and he was pleased that his children were doing well in school.

Thobias' oldest son was finishing high school and wanted desperately to go to college. His teacher had encouraged him to go to Salatiga, Central Java. If he could pass the entrance test, maybe he could get a scholarship to study at Satya Wacana Christian University. What an impossible dream! Just to get there would take two days by horseback to Kupang, three days by boat to Java, and an overnight trip by bus from Surabaya to Salatiga.

Thobias didn't know how he would manage, but he told his son that he would send him to college at Satya Wacana. Everyone in the village laughed at the idea, for it was practically unheard of to send a child to college, let alone to one on the island of Java. Thobias kept his thoughts to himself and prayed for power equal to the task. He began by selling all of his cattle—a very bold step for a cattle farmer in a remote village of Timor in those days. As family members heard of his dream, they began to help too, and eventually Thobias had collected enough money for his son's trip to Java.

What a leap of faith to be confident of what he could not see! Today, not one but *five* of Thobias' children have university degrees because he dared to trust when others could not.

"Papa" is what I call him, for he became my father-in-law when I married the oldest son he had sent off to college in Java.

For Reflection

1. What is demanded of us when we, like Thobias, take the road less traveled?
2. Reflect upon a time in your own life when you were rewarded for trusting the unknown. What risks did you take at the time?

3. What steps can we take to help build up our trust in the unfamiliar?

When we confront the unknown, give us courage, for faith assures us of your presence and companionship along the way.

God's Provision

However, we don't want to offend them, so go down to the lake and throw in a line. Open the mouth of the first fish you catch, and you will find a large silver coin. Take it and pay the tax for both of us.

—Matthew 17:27

LATE ONE EVENING, our relatives in Timor phoned to tell us that my father-in-law was experiencing severe chest pains.

"We don't know what to do," they sighed. "What would you suggest?"

"Get him to the hospital!" my husband shouted into the phone. It took several more urgent phone calls to our relatives to make sure that they did.

When Papa was finally admitted to the hospital, his attending physician asked if he had ever consulted a doctor about his chest pains.

"No," he answered, resigned to his fate. "I went to a prayer team instead, and they prayed for me."

Not long after that, a cousin of ours needed surgery and was obviously worried about not being able to afford it. My husband asked if he was carrying any kind of health insurance.

"Oh, no," he replied. "That would mean I didn't trust in God's provision!"

At about that time a close friend from church was heading off to North Sumatra for a national martial arts competition. As he said good-bye to us, he pleaded, "Please pray for my success," as though our prayers would bring him a gold medal.

What's wrong here? All that we have comes from God, and God answers prayer, but should prayer end in words or in action? Does trusting in God's provision somehow exonerate us from going to the doctor, investing in insurance, and training for competitions? Does God expect us to sit idly by, just trusting in his provision and praying to him fervently, or does he expect us to act upon the guidance he gives us by using the brains and resources he has already provided?

Did Jesus just hand the coin to Peter, or did he make him work for it?

For Reflection

1. What are the dangers in blindly trusting that God will provide whatever we want if we pray hard enough?
2. Describe a time when God's provision differed from your expectations. In what way did it differ, and how did you come to terms with that?
3. Think of a time when you needed to work hard for what God had provided.

Make us mindful, Father, that even though you supply all that we need, you often expect us to be an active participant in getting it.

Chapter 2
God's Nature and Will

> If God were small enough to be understood,
> He would not be big enough to be worshiped.[2]
> —Evelyn Underhill

Calling God Father

> See how very much our Father loves us, for he calls us his children, and that is what we are! But the people who belong to this world don't recognize that we are God's children because they don't know him.
> —1 John 3:1

WHAT WE CALL others shows the kind of relationship we share with them. When my father-in-law met me for the first time and he said, "Just call me Papa," somehow our relationship seemed closer. So too when God calls us his children and Jesus refers to him as our Father in heaven, we know that we are a cherished and integral part of God's family.

How Muslims refer to God also shows the kind of relationship they share with their creator. Allah is referred to by many names—*the King, the Mighty, the Holy, the Protector, the Source of Peace,* and so on. Allah has ninety-nine names, it is claimed, and according to the Hadrith (traditional accounts about what Muhammad did or said), those who know them all will go to Paradise.

18 Light for the Journey

There may be ninety-nine names for God, but "Father" is not one of them. "How can God be a father?" a Muslim student once asked me. "He was never married." To put God on a par with us by calling him *Father* was disrespectful in her eyes. Indeed, doing so is condemned by the Qur'an.

When we call God's name as Christians, we are not calling a remote and distant power that tests us and punishes us through earthquakes and tsunamis. Our God is the triune God who so loved the world that he sent his only Son, not to save those who memorize ninety-nine names but all those who call on his name.

For Reflection

1. How would you answer the Muslim student who asked, "How can God be a father? He was never married."
2. What are some attributes of God that make him a "father" to you?

3. How would you explain the Trinity to a Muslim who claims that by worshiping the Father, Son, and Holy Spirit, you are worshiping three gods, not one?

Father, how privileged we are to be called your children! Thank you for supporting and sustaining us with your love.

Talking with God

> Always be joyful. Never stop praying. Be thankful in all circumstances, for this is God's will for you who belong to Christ Jesus.
> —1 Thessalonians 5:16-18

THE CALL TO prayer from the mosque can be so melodious when performed by a professional muezzin. How different it is, though, when chanted by an old man who coughs halfway through or by a child who has been given the chance to practice and obviously enjoys hearing his voice over the loudspeaker.

Our house in Central Java sits on a wooded hillside, and from that vantage point there is no escape. Five times a day we hear the call to prayer from five different mosques. The first call rudely awakens us around 4:00 A.M. Within half an hour it is absolute bedlam—a cacophony of calls blaring forth from five different loudspeakers. Even Muslims agree that it's noisy. Former President of Indonesia, Abdurrahman Wahid (Gus Dur), with tongue in cheek, once lamented that since the Almighty is not deaf, Muslims must think he is awfully far away.[3]

Actually, observing the way in which people pray can tell us quite a bit about the God to whom they pray. For Muslims, Allah is an exacting God who not only expects his followers to pray five times a day but to do it in the correct way—facing Mecca, wearing prescribed clothing, using the Arabic language, and prostrating themselves before him. A Muslim gains merit through prayer. God harshly judges those who do not pray or who fail to do it properly.

For Christians, on the contrary, God is not an exacting deity but a loving heavenly Father who expects his followers to be joyful and thankful. He asks them to pray and welcomes their prayers but does not specify the number of times they must pray. Nor does he stipulate the clothing they must wear, the position they must take, the words they must speak, or even the language they must use. For those who belong to Christ, what inhabits the heart is more important than what meets the eye.

For Reflection

1. Christians are told to pray without ceasing. What does that mean to you?
2. As a Christian, why do you pray? What is your motive? How does this differ from a Muslim's motive?
3. What should your attitude be as you come before God in prayer?

Thank you, Lord, for the relationship you have established with us and for the privilege of coming to you in prayer.

Father Knows Best

> When you pray, don't babble on and on as people of other religions do. They think their prayers are answered merely by repeating their words again and again. Don't be like them, for your Father knows exactly what you need even before you ask him!
>
> —Matthew 6:7-8

A FEW YEARS ago my retina detached, and I had to undergo several operations to try to save the sight in my right eye.

A friend at our Indonesian church shook her head in dismay when she heard the news. "Well, if you had prayed harder," she said, "you wouldn't have needed surgery!"

Her assertion surprised me. Was it because I hadn't prayed hard enough that I needed eye surgery and eventually lost my sight?

Another member of our congregation came up to me one Sunday after the service and lamented that her son had not passed our university entrance test.

"I just don't understand it," she said. "Why didn't God want to answer my prayers?"

If God knows what we need before we ask him, surely we know even better. "Restore my sight!" (without surgery) or "Give me a good mark on the test!" (whether I study enough or not). If I don't get what I want, it must mean that either I am not praying hard enough or God is not listening hard enough.

When Jesus prayed "Take this cup from me!" on the cross, did he not also say, "Nevertheless, not my will but yours be done"? Have we not been taught to do the same?

For Reflection

1. What are people insinuating about the nature of God when they claim that we would not be sick or need surgery if we had prayed harder?
2. How would you answer such claims?
3. Why should we pray at all if God knows exactly what we need, anyway?

Oh loving heavenly Father, whose greatness and majesty are beyond our comprehension, forgive us when we call on you to do our bidding. Teach us to accept your will and appreciate what comes from your hand, knowing that the answers you give are always far wiser than the requests we make.

God's Will

> He has showered his kindness on us, along with all wisdom and understanding.
> —Ephesians 1:8

WHEN A TRAGEDY occurs, people like to point fingers and play the blame game. So it is with natural disasters too. When the tsunami struck Aceh on December 26, 2004, Indonesians shook their heads in wonder and asked who was responsible for a disaster of such magnitude. What had caused God to unleash such anger upon his people? All sorts of reasons were proposed:

- God was warning Muslims not to be so proud and arrogant just because they were the majority in Indonesia.
- God was cursing the Acehnese people because they were never satisfied and wanted to break away from Indonesia.
- God had been angered by the Christmas celebrations of Christians the day before.

- God was punishing the Acehnese because tourists had held beach parties near a cemetery, a sacred place.
- God was enraged because Indonesians had neglected him and become immoral.
- God was punishing the nation because of the sins of its leaders.

Those of us who are Christian had a hard time accepting such accusations. Our God, after all, is not a God of revenge but a God of love. Is it God's will for people to face death and destruction, or is it God's will for all people to find joy in his presence?

For Reflection

1. Recall a natural disaster in your own area of the world. In what different ways did people interpret God's will at the time?
2. Do you believe that God uses natural disasters like the 2011 earthquake in Christchurch, New Zealand, or the tsunami in Japan to correct and admonish his people? Why or why not?
3. How would you respond to those who blamed the December 26th tsunami in Aceh on Christians for partying too much the day before?

Give us the courage, wisdom, and understanding to face the adversities that come our way in life. Remind us that you are with us and will most surely see us through.

The Silent Hand of God

> The heavens proclaim the glory of God. The skies display his craftsmanship.
> —Psalms 19:1

THE 2004 TSUNAMI turned the province of Aceh on the northern tip of Sumatra into a wasteland. The huge waves which swept over the land obliterated the people's homes, markets, and ways of life.

In Aceh, the only Indonesian province allowed to practice traditional sharia law, the mosques were what sheltered local Muslims from the cataclysm. The main Baiturrahman Mosque was one of the only buildings left standing in the capital city of Bande Aceh. Until today, the Achenese have credited the survival of this mosque to divine intervention.

Many survivors say God's wrath destroyed arrogant and greedy people but protected his house of worship. Although a Christian friend of ours contends that the main mosque was spared because the architect happened to be a Christian, most Achenese say it was because the mosque was well-built. After all, people would not dare to be corrupt with funds for a mosque, and those who built this place of worship had their hearts in the right place. Therefore, the mosque was spared.

Normally we, like David the psalmist, think of God as a positive force, as our rock and our redeemer. When God releases his power and reveals himself through such natural disasters, however, what are we to think? How are we to explain such destruction?

None of us can understand the mind of God. We do know, however, that he is trustworthy and can be taken at his word. If God was able to create the world, has displayed his craftsmanship throughout the centuries, and continues to reveal his natural power to this extent today, should we not trust that he can also help us deal with the more mundane problems we face in life from day to day?

For Reflection

1. Do you believe that God's wrath destroys arrogant and greedy people but protects his house of worship?
2. How would you respond to the friend who believes that the mosque was spared because the architect happened to be a Christian?
3. How do you interpret the nature and will of God when disasters strike?

As frightened and awed as we are by your natural power, oh God, we take comfort in your promise to be with us and never to abandon us.

What's It Like?

"…So tell us, whose wife will she be in the resurrection? For all seven were married to her." Jesus replied, "Your mistake is that you don't know the Scriptures, and you don't know the power of God."
—Matthew 22:28-29

EVEN THOUGH JESUS came, lived among us, and taught us about God's nature and will, we humans have a hard time envisioning what we have not experienced. The only thing we can do is to compare the unknown (such as life in heaven) to the known (life on earth).

The conversation between the Sadducees and Jesus reminds me of a conversation I had with a twelve-year-old Indian village girl who wanted to know what life was like in the United States. Our conversation went like this:

Kamala: Have the monsoons started yet in your country?
Me: No, we don't have monsoons. It rains now and then all year long.
Kamala: How can you grow rice if you don't have a monsoon?

Me:	We don't grow rice.
Kamala:	*What?* Well, what do you eat your curry with if you don't have rice?
Me:	We don't eat rice and curry. We eat meat and vegetables, fish and eggs.
Kamala:	Can bananas grow in your country?
Me:	Yes, in parts. But not where I live.
Kamala:	What do you do without banana leaves to eat off of?
Me:	We only use plates.
Kamala:	How can you clean all those plates if you don't have servants?
Me:	We just do. Some people have machines that clean the plates.
Kamala:	Now tell me, how can a machine clean a plate?

Some things we will never understand, and we simply have to leave it at that. We probably have no better understanding of God's word and power than the Sadducees did. Instead of concerning ourselves with the future and the mysteries of heaven, then, it might be better to focus on our relationship with God and whether or not we are making his priorities our own.

For Reflection

1. What would you have asked Jesus about heaven if you had been there that day with the Sadducees?
2. What have your own experiences taught you about the nature, power, and will of God?
3. What are God's priorities for your life right now? How do you know?

Forgive us for being so self-absorbed and shortsighted, oh God of wisdom and might. Remind us that you make your power available to us as we make your priorities our own.

Chapter 3
Our Identity

We perceive the world not as it is, but as we are.[4]
—David G. Myers

Who Are You?

> As a face is reflected in water, so the heart reflects the real person.
> —Proverbs 27:19

WHO ARE YOU? Who are you really, deep in your heart? It's an important question each of us as Christians should ask ourselves as we journey through life.

In Indonesia, your name gives us a clue about who you are. If it's *Made*, you are the second child of a Balinese family. If it's *Soeharto*, you are probably Javanese, and if it's *Sirait*, you're Batak. From your skin color, hair texture, and facial features we can usually guess your ethnic group, and from your dress we can sometimes tell your religion. If you are wearing a jilbab (headscarf), undoubtedly you are a Muslim, and if you are wearing a cross, you are a Christian.

Who are you? Perhaps you define yourself in terms of a relationship ("I'm Daniel's wife." "I'm Peter's mother."). Then again, you might believe "I am what I do." I'm a teacher, a nurse, a carpenter, a lawyer—until you retire or are deprived of your role and therefore your identity. What then?

Identity matters. When we don't know who we really are, we lack self-worth, self-respect, and self-dignity. It is also through our identity that we see the world. As noted social psychologist David Myers so aptly put it, "We perceive the world not as it is, but as we are."[5] How we perceive it makes a world of difference.

For Reflection

1. When people ask you who you are, how do you answer?
2. How has your own identity affected the way in which you perceive the world?
3. What would you like other people to see in you, reflected from your heart? What would you like to be said about you in a eulogy?

Help us to value ourselves as you do, oh Lord, and, in so doing, value and respect others.

What's in a Name?

"What is your name?" the man asked. He replied, "Jacob."
"Your name will no longer be Jacob," the man told him.
"From now on you will be called Israel, because you have fought with God and with men and have won."
—Genesis 32:27-28

WHETHER AN INDONESIAN has one name, like Sukarno, or six, like my husband, Daniel Daud Jonathan Fritz Johannes Kameo, each name conveys meaning. By looking at people's names, we can tell quite a bit about them —their ethnic background, their religion, and often their birth order or status.

Every name has a story to tell. It not only carries identity but often also conveys the character of the one who bears it. Most Indonesians believe that names hold power and carry weight. When a colleague asked Daniel what the second "D" in his name stood for, he told him "Daud" (*David* in Indonesian).

"Whoa!" the colleague exclaimed. "*Daniel* and *Daud*—a prophet and a king? Isn't that too heavy a name for you to carry around?"

Names can bring good luck or bad luck. When sickness or misfortune strikes a child, Indonesians often blame the name given to the child and change it. Changing names for better luck is not limited to humans, either. When a train named Empu Jaya was recently involved in three accidents, Indonesian railway managers decided the name was too powerful, and they renamed it Progo to restore its image.

For Reflection

1. Do you believe that names have power and that changing a name can change one's fate?
2. In the Old Testament, Jacob's name was changed to Israel. Name some other people in the Bible who underwent name changes. What did their new names mean?
3. What does your name mean? Why is it important to you?

For calling us by name, redeeming us, and claiming us for your own, we give you thanks, oh Lord.

My Dumb Daughter

> "What is the price of five sparrows—two copper coins? Yet God does not forget a single one of them. And the very hairs on your head are all numbered. So don't be afraid; you are more valuable to God than a whole flock of sparrows."
> —Luke 12:6-7

WHEN OUR SON was small and both of us were teaching full time, we interviewed potential nannies to look after him a few hours a day. Several women applied for the job. Among the applicants was a young woman whose Javanese mother had brought her to our house to be interviewed.

Speaking to me in Bahasa Indonesia, the mother introduced her to me by saying, "This is Tri, my dumb daughter."

Well, I thought, if she's dumb, she's certainly not the person I want to hire to look after my son!

Only later did I realize that I had misinterpreted her words. From my Western perspective, I had expected candidates to show their worth and to prove that they were well-qualified for the job.

In Javanese culture, though, modesty is extremely important. The mother had just been doing her best to appear humble.

How people measure self-worth varies from culture to culture. For some it is measured by good looks or achievement; for others it is measured by character or how well one relates to others. Thankfully, God does not measure our worth by earthly standards. God values us just as we are because we belong to him. In Christ we are made worthy.

For Reflection

1. How does the value we place on ourselves affect our outlook on life?
2. What is the difference between unworthiness and worthlessness?
3. Does humility require that we put ourselves down?

Oh Lord, when looks, personal success, and performance become the measure by which we evaluate ourselves and others, remind us that our true worth lies not in earthly standards but in our identity with Christ. May the knowledge that we belong to him enable us to face life with courage.

Being Yourself

So all of us who have had that veil removed can see and reflect the glory of the Lord. And the Lord—who is the Spirit—makes us more and more like him as we are changed into his glorious image.

—2 Corinthians 3:18

ON THE INDONESIAN island of Bali, dance performances have been an important part of the Hindu religion and culture for over a thousand years. The masks the dancers wear are not just costume accessories. They themselves hold sacred power. Some help the wearers to make contact with their ancestors, and others help them to harness supernatural forces. The dancers are no longer themselves, for they are changed and transformed by the masks they wear.

Like these Balinese dancers, many of us go through life wearing masks that hide our real identity. Instead of being true to ourselves and following our instincts, we pretend to be what we are not. If we do this often enough, we become changed and transformed by the masks we wear. We begin to believe that we have become what we are not.

God created us with a purpose and has endowed each of us with unique abilities and talents. It is important to know what that purpose is and to develop those God-given abilities and talents. Deceiving ourselves and others by trying to be what we are not only makes it harder for us to serve God in the way he intended.

For Reflection

1. How does the way you see yourself affect the way you live? Give examples.
2. What masks have you worn which have prevented you from being true to yourself?
3. In what ways do you find it difficult to be the person God created you to be?

Ensure us of your constant love for us just as we are, creator God. Help us to become the people you have created us to be so that we might reach our God-given potential and reflect your glory.

A Chosen People

> But you are not like that, for you are a chosen people. You are royal priests, a holy nation, God's very own possession. As a result, you can show others the goodness of God, for he called you out of the darkness into his wonderful light.
> —1 Peter 2:9

HOW WOULD YOU feel if you had been told from birth that you were the scum of the earth? How would it affect your outlook on life if you were so impure that other people could not even touch you? This is the way it is for over 100 million outcast Hindus in India.

When I taught English at a large Christian girls' school in South India, about half of my students were outcasts—Untouchables or Dalits. It did not take long to discover why so many had become Christian. Christianity had offered them a whole new self-image. It had changed them from the inside out. You could tell by the way they looked at you. You could tell by the way they talked and the way they walked.

As Christians, they came to know that no matter what society said, they were a chosen people, created in the image of God. They belonged to God, and every single one of them mattered. They no longer lived in fear, for they trusted that God would lovingly direct them and keep them in his care. Empowered through Christ, they had become what Peter Gomes calls "the human expression of the Divine hope."[6]

The most enthusiastic Christians I know are converts. They simply radiate the goodness of God. Never for a moment do they take their faith for granted. Never for a moment should we.

For Reflection

1. Christianity gives us a different identity. As we see God within us and working through us, how does it change the way we look at others?
2. What does it mean to love others as we love ourselves? How do we accomplish that?
3. In what specific way has another Christian been the "human expression of the Divine hope" for you in your life?

Nourished and empowered by your love, may we live out our Christian identity with courage, hope, and compassion.

In His Image

> So God created human beings in his own image. In the image of God he created them; male and female he created them.
> —Genesis 1:27

AS A WOMAN, I have often felt fortunate that I was not born into a Jewish family at the time of Jesus. How limited I would have been by Jewish law and tradition! When I began working for the church overseas, however, I soon learned that even in our own day, women have been subjected to laws and traditions that make them question just how equally they were created in the image of God.

As a lay missionary to India in the 1960s, centuries after Jesus befriended Mary Magdalene, Mary and Martha of Bethany, Joanna, Susanna, Lydia, Priscilla, Dorcas, and Phoebe, I soon learned how inferior I was to men. Women teachers at our girls' school used to speak with pride when they gave birth to a boy but with apology and regret when they gave birth to a girl. Through the Indian dowry system, boys brought wealth to the family when they got married. Girls, on the other hand, became a financial burden to the family. Even I, as a Western woman, began to question my own value when a young man on the train told me, "I thank God every day that I was not born a woman."

Fifteen years later when I was teaching in Hong Kong, I wondered just what it would take to convince women that they were created in the image of God and that God showed no partiality. At birth, a girl was referred to as a piece of tile whereas a boy was referred to as a piece of jade. It was the girls who always had to drop out and work to support their brothers through school. As they grew up and married, they were expected to play a secondary role in the household as well.

We are told in Galatians 3:28 that faith in Christ transcends differences in race and gender. Unfortunately, societal values often have a way of trumping that. How did women missionaries in Hong Kong feel when only the men of our mission groups were invited to attend meetings with the Chinese church? The women were invited too—but only for dinner after all of the decisions had been made. The practice I found in a village in North Sumatra was even more wrenching. Imagine my surprise when I attended services in one village only to be told that, as a woman, I was not allowed to take Holy Communion. Only the men of the congregation were allowed to do that; women were relegated to the washing up afterwards.

Should it surprise us, then, when we find Christian women around the world who say they feel inferior and have trouble identifying themselves as people created in the image of God, loved and forgiven?

For Reflection

1. How did Jesus show that he valued women? In what specific ways did he demonstrate concern for them?
2. What is your own national church currently doing to improve the lives of women around the world?

3. What other forms of inequity, if any, need to be addressed by the church?

   Oh Lord, help us to remember that all people are made in your image and deserve to be valued as much as you value them.

Duck Paws

But as I looked at everything I had worked so hard to accomplish, it was all so meaningless – like chasing the wind. There was nothing really worthwhile anywhere.
—Ecclesiastes 2:11

"HOW MANY PATIENTS today?" our waiter asked as we entered a restaurant in Kowloon, Hong Kong. Puzzled by his choice of words, I said nothing but followed along after the other English teachers from Lutheran Middle School who had decided to eat out instead of having the usual school cafeteria fare.

As our waiter handed us menus, I asked, "What would you recommend today?"

"Well, this dish with duck paws is delicious," he replied.

"Duck paws?" I asked with a smile.

"He obviously didn't study English from *you*," a Chinese colleague whispered in my ear. "That's why we need native speakers of English like you teaching at our school. What would we do without you?"

It was heartwarming to hear her say that, for sometimes lay missionaries who teach English as a second language abroad wonder if it is time well spent. Church colleagues who work in mission hospitals save lives on a day-to-day basis. Those who build wells can count the number they have helped to dig by the end of the month. But those who teach English feel a bit like the pyramid builders must have felt. We work day in and day out without seeing much progress. Just as it took years to build the pyramids, so also it takes years to create a fluent speaker of English.

As we teach our students the difference between patients and customers, or paws and feet, we wonder if any of it is sinking in. Then one day a former student drops by to tell us that because of her fluency in English she has won a scholarship to study in Australia or is being sent to an international conference in Paris. When we finally see the finished pyramid, we suddenly become aware of the differences we have made and the worth of what we do.

For Reflection

1. How would you respond to a member of your home congregation who asks, "How do you justify calling yourself a missionary? You only teach English!"
2. How do you judge the value of the work you do?
3. What makes a Christian worthy?

Help us to see meaning and value in the work we feel called by you to do.

Dressing As a Christian

> Above all, clothe yourselves with love, which binds us all together in perfect harmony.
> —Colossians 3:14

WHEN I BEGAN teaching at Satya Wacana Christian University in Central Java, I could never tell whether my students were Christian, Buddhist, Hindu, or Muslim. They all dressed the same. Most likely, a student from Bali was Hindu, and an Indonesian of Chinese descent was Christian or Buddhist, but other than that I had no way of knowing their religious identities.

One semester this inability of mine got the best of me when I asked an active student in the front row of my Christian ethics class to be my assistant—to help prepare, duplicate, and distribute materials, set up the equipment before class, and alert me to the needs of her classmates. Only at the end of the semester did I discover that I had asked a Muslim to be my assistant in a Christian ethics class. How badly I felt, knowing that this must have caused her embarrassment in front of her Muslim classmates.

Dressing As a Christian

After 9/11, when Indonesian Muslims were advised to assert their identity and observe Islamic dress, many of our female students began wearing Muslim head scarves. As if to counter this, Christian students began wearing crosses. Suddenly it became much easier to tell who was what.

In reality, however, being a Christian does not depend upon what we put on. As Christians we are not defined by what we wear but how we act. "And they'll know we are Christians by our love," we sing. May our actions so reflect God's glory that others recognize us for what we are.

For Reflection

1. How has God manifested his love through you recently?
2. In what ways do you demonstrate your identity in Christ?
3. Do you believe that you can broadcast your faith without wearing a cross or ever saying a word?

Help us to reveal our identity to the world by putting on the love of Christ.

Chapter 4
Living in Grace

The Law tells me how crooked I am;
Grace comes along and straightens me out.[7]
—Dwight L. Moody

The Flagellant

> But if we confess our sins to him, he is faithful and just to forgive us our sins and to cleanse us from all wickedness.
> —1 John 1:9

IT WAS BEASTLY hot that day as missionary friends and I trudged up the sacred mountain at Kotappa Konda, Andhra Pradesh, South India. We were headed for the venerated Sri Trikoteswara Swami Temple, where Hindus were participating in a fertility rite during the festival of Mahasivaratri.

On we walked among brightly painted cows, decorated carts, and throngs of Mahasivaratri pilgrims. Suddenly, without any warning, a flagellant leapt out in front of us. Jumping and

dancing, the dark-skinned torturer lashed his body again and again with a long whip. Blood glistened on his chest. He was earning merit by punishing himself for his sins, and the pilgrims who tossed coins onto his tin plate were earning merit by giving alms to this well-meaning flagellant.

My heart went out to this man who was suffering so unnecessarily to earn forgiveness through his public penance. Think of it: as Christians, we do not have to punish ourselves, wash in a holy river, avoid certain foods, fast, go on a pilgrimage, or sacrifice an animal to make ourselves right with God. That has already been done for us through the death and resurrection of Jesus Christ. Instead of living by rituals and regulations, we live in freedom through God's forgiveness and grace.

How hard some people work to earn God's forgiveness! How easy it is for those of us in Christ to take the gift of God's forgiveness and grace for granted!

For Reflection

1. So often the most active and enthusiastic Christians in Asia and elsewhere are new converts. Why do you think this is the case?
2. What is worse—to work so hard to set things right with God or to take the gift of God's forgiveness and grace for granted?
3. In gratitude for what God has done, how should we respond to the gift of salvation? List some things we and our congregations should be doing.

Merciful God, forgive us when the familiarity of the good news prevents us from appreciating the gift of your forgiveness and grace as we ought.

Free Indeed!

> So Christ has truly set us free. Now make sure that you stay free, and don't get tied up again in slavery to the law.
> —Galatians 5:1

AS OUR FAMILY was preparing for Christmas last year, we heard a cleric shouting over the loudspeaker at our local mosque. "There is no savior! God keeps track of everything you do, and what you do determines whether you go to heaven or to hell," he declared. "Everything you do is recorded in a book of deeds; every action, big and small, is on record. So don't think you can sin and get away with it! No one will free you from your sins. Again, I say there is no savior!"

His message jarred me out of my complacency. What a different beat non-Christians dance to. What a burden! They have to work so hard to earn God's favor and salvation. As Christians, we have already received God's approval, and we are saved through Jesus Christ.

A good Muslim friend of mine once said to me, "It must be nice to be a Christian. You don't have to do anything. You're free!" And, you know, she's right. We don't have to pray five times a day, fast, or make a trip to Mecca. We don't have to try harder and harder to please an angry God. As another friend of mine put it, "They are trying to buy their way to heaven. We Christians already have the ticket."

What is our response to this incredible gift of freedom?

For Reflection

1. Jesus said that he did not come to abolish the law. Does that mean, then, that we are still expected to obey the rules and regulations of the Old Testament? Why or why not?
2. Why do we keep on sinning if faith in Christ has set us free from sin's power over us?
3. What is the purpose of doing good works if we are already saved by grace?

May our lives so reflect your glory that others come to know of your grace and love.

Just Tell Me What To Do!

> For if you are trying to make yourselves right with God by keeping the law, you have been cut off from Christ! You have fallen away from God's grace.
> —Galatians 5:4

OUR SON, PETER, grew up in Java playing with both Muslim and Christian children. One day, at the ripe old age of eleven, he declared, "You know, Mom, Islam is so much easier than Christianity!"

"How's that?" I asked.

"Everything is so clear, that's why! It's all written down in black and white. Just follow the rules. You know exactly what to do. But Christianity? It's all so vague and confusing!"

Vague and confusing? I had never thought of it that way before. Indeed, Paul says that Christ has set us free, but being free does not necessarily make life any easier, does it? We may feel more comfortable with a religion that tells us exactly what to do and not to do. We may feel more contented with a religion that allows us to earn God's favor. We may feel more satisfied with a religion that we can control for our own benefit—a religion that allows us to say, "I failed the test because I didn't pray enough."

For those who follow the law, the choice has already been made. We who choose to follow Christ, however, have already been put right with God. If we stick to the law, Christ is of no use to us, Paul explains. If we try to be put right with God, we cut ourselves off from Christ because we are saying that we do not need a Savior. We can do it by ourselves.

For Reflection

1. What makes Christianity a difficult religion to understand?
2. What would be the benefits of a religion that allowed you to earn God's favor?
3. What problems arise when law-keeping becomes an end in itself?

Forgive us, Lord, when we try to earn your favor instead of accepting Jesus as our Savior.

Earning God's Favor

> And since it is through God's kindness, then it is not by their good works. For in that case, God's grace would not be what it really is—free and undeserved.
> —Romans 11:6

A COUSIN FROM the island of Timor was visiting us in Salatiga a few years ago. As we were driving home from town one afternoon, he suddenly remarked that it was obvious to him that we were very good people.

"Why do you say that?" I asked curiously.

"Well, just look!" he exclaimed. "You are healthy, you are well-educated, you both have excellent jobs, and you have a beautiful home of our own. Obviously, God has showered his favor upon you!"

"We do feel blessed," I replied, not sure where the conversation was leading.

"It just goes to show," he continued, "that when you walk in the light the way God wants you to live, he blesses you. Praise the Lord!"

What was wrong with this picture? Indeed, we felt blessed for the way our lives were going, but was God showering his favor upon us because of our good behavior? Was the quality of our health, education, jobs, and home living proof that we were good people? Had we somehow earned it?

When a thief broke into our home a few months later, we lost money, jewelry, a camera, and a laptop. Did this reversal of fortunes somehow indicate that we had made a detour through the darkness and had failed to satisfy God? When things go badly for us personally, is it because our actions have failed to please God, and we are being punished for it?

If grace is a free and undeserved gift, why is God rewarding us when we are good and punishing us when we are bad?

For Reflection

1. What would you have said in response to the cousin from Timor?
2. If grace is a free gift, as Paul tells us, why do we keep trying to earn it or act as if we have earned it?
3. How should we respond to God's gift of grace?

May our lives reflect the gratefulness we feel for your overwhelming gift of grace.

To Eat or Not To Eat

> But you must be careful so that your freedom does not cause others with a weaker conscience to stumble.
> —1 Corinthians 8:9

ONE DAY, SEVERAL Indian friends and I were driving back to Rajahmundry from the tribal village of Rampachodavaram with Hilda Karcher, a longtime Lutheran missionary to India. We stopped near a temple to stretch our legs and take pictures along the side of the road. It was nearly lunchtime, and I was hungry.

As we chatted in Telugu with the people who stopped to greet us, two women came by and graciously shared some of the provisions they were carrying. I was grateful for their generosity, but Hilda looked concerned.

"Thank them, but don't eat it," she advised.

"Why not?" I asked, for the food seemed fresh and appealing enough.

"Because most likely it has been offered to idols," she explained.

Idols? Was Hilda worried about what would happen to us if we ate food offered to idols? As she nodded in the direction

of the others, it dawned on me. She was worried about what the new Indian converts traveling with us would think if we ate food which had been offered to Hindu idols. After all, they might not yet be as secure in their faith as we were.

Paul tells us that Christ has set us free from sin and from following a long list of rules and regulations. We are free, then, not to do as we like but to make our own choices. In making those choices, we need to be sensitive to the way in which our actions are perceived by others. It is not only what we do that is important but the way it affects those around us.

For Reflection

1. Reflect on a time when what you were doing was misinterpreted by others. What happened?
2. What freedoms have others forfeited so that you would not be adversely affected? What freedoms do you forfeit for the sake of others?
3. How can we learn to become more sensitive to the needs of others around us?

Father of all people and nations, help us to become more sensitive not only to what we do but to the way our actions might be perceived by others.

Chapter 5
Walking in the Light

There are two ways of spreading light:
To be the candle or the mirror that reflects it.[8]
—Edith Wharton

Dulled by Familiarity

> There is much more we would like to say about this, but it is difficult to explain, especially since you are spiritually dull and don't seem to listen.
> —Hebrews 5:11

"EEEYAEEEYAEEE!" THE SIREN screamed as the ambulance sped along the street below my third floor classroom in Kowloon, Hong Kong. As if the ordinary street noise wasn't bad enough, we had to contend with sirens all day long, for our school was not only located across the street from a hospital but right between a private ambulance service on the one side and the fire department on the other. When I complained about the noise to my Chinese colleagues, though, you would have thought I was from Planet X.

What noise?

What noise, indeed! They had become so used to it over the years that they no longer even heard it.

How often we become dulled by the ordinary. When I was having my tonsils out at our mission hospital in India, for example, the nurses were surprised that I had noticed the monkey sitting in the tree outside my window. For them, monkeys were as common as spiders.

A similar thing happened when I was serving as a library consultant for a Christian college in the Palestinian Territories. The first day I nearly jumped out of my skin at the sudden repetitive screeching outside the window. The librarian chuckled. After all, it was only the hee-hawing of a donkey.

Oh how quickly our senses become dulled by the familiar!

Have our senses become dulled by the familiarity of the "old, old story" as well, or does it continue to arouse us and excite us? Comfortably settled into our ruts, how easy it is to become spiritually dull. Perhaps we too could benefit from the call for spiritual growth.

For Reflection

1. To what have you become so accustomed that you no longer notice it?
2. What is the danger of becoming dulled and insensitive to the good news?
3. What can we do to prevent this from happening?

May we never become so dulled by our familiarity with the gospel that we take the good news for granted.

Waiting in Hope

> And may the Lord make your love for one another and for all people grow and overflow, just as our love for you overflows. May he, as a result, make your hearts strong, blameless, and holy as you stand before God our Father when our Lord Jesus comes again with all his holy people.
> —1 Thessalonians 3:12-13

OUR BAGS WERE packed, and we were checking our supplies for the rugged journey across West Timor to the remote village of Oepoli, my husband's ancestral home. After twenty-eight years of marriage, I had never been there and still hadn't met most of our relatives in Amfoang Utara.

We were to stop at two villages along the way, Taen and Binaus. As we pulled out of Kupang, relatives in Taen and Binaus were preparing for our arrival. They had called everyone with the name of Kameo from seven surrounding villages to come down to the road to meet us. They had sent out scouts during the day to check on our progress. They had prepared welcome dances, a formal program, and a meal for everyone.

Waiting in Hope 69

When our convoy finally arrived, the whole family gave a sigh of relief. They had been waiting in full costume for eight hours just in case we should happen to arrive early!

As Christians, all of us wait in hope. The season of Advent makes us especially aware of this. We are waiting to celebrate something that happened over 2,000 years ago, but that's not all. We are also waiting and preparing ourselves for Christ's coming again. Luke 21:34-36 and the reading from 1 Thessalonians tell us how we should wait.

For Reflection

1. What parallels can you draw between the way the Timorese villagers waited and the way we wait during the season of Advent?
2. How are we supposed to fill our time as we wait for Christ's second coming?
3. Waiting in hope in a world like ours is not easy. In what way has Christ equipped us to wait in hope?

Fill us with the courage, strength, and hope we need to witness to the one who came into the world at Christmas and will come again.

Joy in an Indian Village

~~~

You will show me the way of life, granting me the joy of your presence and the pleasures of living with you forever.
—Psalm 16:11

TIRED FARMERS WERE trudging home from the fields with their water buffalo as we lurched into a South Indian village that December afternoon. Ragged children were parading along the dusty road, singing Telugu Christmas carols. After each song, a boy would shout out a Bible verse through a homemade megaphone. Seeing our Jeep rattle to a stop, the children cheered and swarmed around us. Only the water buffalo paid us no heed.

As we made the rounds of the village and entered each thatched-roof hut, family members tethered their animals to the side and brought out the only piece of furniture they owned—a rope bed. As we sat down on it, the children and their elders, in good Indian style, sat cross-legged on the dirt floor in front of us. A boy who had learned to read was asked to read us the Christmas story in Telugu, and then everyone broke into songs of joy and gladness.

In this remote village no one had ever heard of Santa Claus or "I'm dreaming of a white Christmas." There was no need to remind them of the real reason for the season because it was the only one they knew. Yes, I was missing my family on the other side of the world, along with Christmas trees, home-baked cookies, colorfully wrapped presents, and snow. This year, though, I had the lowing of cattle and the touch of a baby goat to remind me of that very first Christmas. Was there any better way to celebrate than to sing and clap and shout the good news with humble Indian villagers?

For Reflection

1. What is the most unusual Advent or Christmas you have ever celebrated? What made it special?
2. What joys and frustrations do you normally feel during the Advent season?
3. What could you do to make the season more meaningful to you this year?

Fill us with joy as we prepare our hearts and minds to receive you, Lord Jesus.

The Sacred and the Secular

> Instead, you must worship Christ as Lord of your life. And if someone asks about your Christian hope, always be ready to explain it.
>
> —1 Peter 3:15

WHEN I WAS growing up in Iowa, my parents never allowed me to believe in Santa Claus. Christmas was the birthday of Jesus, I was told. Jesus was the hope of the world and the reason for the season.

When I began serving in Indonesia, however, I soon discovered that the reason for the season was not always as obvious to Indonesian Christians as it was to my parents. One of the first Christmas cards I received featured Santa Claus jumping out of the Bible. Imagine my surprise when I discovered that the card had been sent to me by a Catholic sister!

It is not all that unusual to see the sacred and the secular served up together in Indonesian churches. On the first Sunday in Advent last year, for example, worshippers in our church looked up to find Santa's stocking hanging in the chancel. The nativity scene at a neighboring church featured Santa praying at the manger.

At my uncle's church in Timor, Santa Claus and Black Piet passed out candy at the Sunday school Christmas pageant. Never mind, of course, that it should have been the elves helping Santa, not St. Nicholas' Black Piet. Who was to know the difference?

Who indeed but the Dutch and the Portuguese, who had brought Christmas to Indonesia in the first place! Indonesians I talk to claim they received Christmas lock, stock, and barrel from their colonizers without knowing which symbols and traditions were sacred and which were secular.

Are Indonesian Christians concerned when they hear their children ask if Santa was one of the disciples? Are they worried if new converts see their hope in Santa Claus as well as in Jesus Christ? Not really. To quote the English writer G. K. Chesterton, "It isn't that they can't see the solution. It's that they can't see the problem."[9]

For Reflection

1. Are some secular holiday symbols more acceptable in the church than others? If so, which ones?
2. What potential problems can you see when churches mix the secular with the sacred?
3. If mixing the sacred and the secular in Indonesian churches is a problem, what kind of a program would you design to remedy the situation?

Lord of life, help us to put our hope in you alone and to be able to explain the reason for our hope when people ask.

Feeling Foolish

> The wise are glad to be instructed, but babbling fools fall flat on their faces.
> —Proverbs 10:8

"ARE YOU ABLE to accept failure?" our mission director asked as I was being interviewed for a job overseas. It seemed like an odd question at the time, but once I began living in another culture, I soon discovered just how easy it was to fail and feel foolish.

For example, during my first year as library director at a Christian university in North Sumatra, I designed a bulletin board on how the library could help students succeed in their studies. To get my point across, I used a striking picture of a wise old owl. It wasn't having the effect I wanted, though. The students shuddered every time they passed it, and it wasn't until a teacher took me aside that I realized why. In Indonesia, owls are mystical, scary creatures. It is not the owl that represents wisdom in Indonesia but the mouse deer.

A few years later I was still making false assumptions. As newly appointed library director at Satya Wacana Christian

University in Central Java, I was moving into my office and had stacked some boxes of books and papers on the floor. To prevent the cleaning lady from throwing them out, I taped a sign on the boxes saying "Jangan dibuang!" (Do not throw away!) The next morning, though, the boxes were gone. When I told my assistant what had happened, he said I shouldn't blame the cleaning woman.

"After all," he explained, "she can't read!"

It had never dawned on me that someone working in a library wouldn't be able to read.

Another reason we fail is because we lack the ordinary skills that people of that culture take for granted. In Hong Kong, for example, people often hang their laundry out the window to dry on poles—a very convenient arrangement for those in high-rise apartments with no yard space. For the Chinese, retrieving the laundry from the pole came as second nature; for a newly arrived American, it was a challenge. The first week I used the long pole, I accidentally allowed it to tilt downwards as I was pulling it in, and the clothes on the end slipped off and fell onto a pole many floors below. What was I to do? I didn't know how to speak Cantonese, and no one in my apartment building spoke English. What signs and gestures could I possibly use to explain to the people several floors down that my underskirt was hanging from their laundry pole?

For those of us who live or work in another culture, making mistakes—sometimes very serious mistakes—come easy. It is learning how to bounce back and forgive ourselves that's hard. If we are "glad to be instructed," though, as Solomon says, then we can be counted among the wise. What an important lesson this is, for in another culture everyone fails at something, even something as simple as using a laundry pole.

For Reflection

1. To err is human. What mistakes do you find hardest to avoid?
2. When you make a serious mistake, do you find it as easy to forgive yourself as you do to forgive others? Why or why not?
3. How does forgiving yourself help in the healing process after you have hurt someone else?

Help us to learn from our mistakes and to forgive ourselves when we fail and look foolish.

Strength Through Weakness

> My grace is all you need. My power works best in weakness.
> —2 Corinthians 12:9

KNOWLEDGE IS POWER, we say. For those who live in a foreign culture, that includes a working knowledge of the language. Give us the speech and vocabulary of a two-year-old and we quickly learn just how weak we are.

I will always remember how embarrassed my Australian friend felt when she was saying good-bye in Indonesian to our university president at the end of a meeting.

"Oh, that's certainly not what you mean!" he exclaimed. "You mean you'll see me next month, don't you?"

"Well, isn't that what I said?" my friend asked.

"No," he said and chuckled. "You said you would see me during your next time of the month." How we all laughed!

Being able to communicate well in the language of the people we serve is essential to those who want to serve effectively in another culture. Learning a new language, though, can be frustrating at best. We know what we want to say, but we seem to make endless slipups and blunders.

Sometimes our mistakes make us feel stupid. I felt that way when I was learning Telugu and asked the Indian doctor sitting next to me at lunch to pass the rice. I couldn't understand why everyone was laughing until they explained to me that I had just asked the doctor to pass the steam.

Sometimes our mistakes make us feel sheepish. That's how I felt when I was learning Indonesian and asked a Javanese student in the back row of my class to open the window. As my students cheered uproariously, I felt my face grow red.

"What did I say?" I asked.

"Instead of 'jendela,' you said 'celana,'" they replied. "You asked him to open his pants!" We all had a good laugh over that one.

Indeed, learning a new language is a humbling experience. Nothing makes us feel more feebleminded than not even being able to talk right. And yet, when mispronunciations or vocabulary mistakes show how weak we are, something positive usually comes of it—joyous humor, good rapport, and warmer relations. Perhaps that is when God steps in and uses our weakness to good advantage.

For Reflection

1. Why is it important for us to recognize our own weaknesses?
2. When do you find it most difficult to admit your weakness?
3. Describe a time when you were unable to handle a situation by yourself and felt God working through you.

Let us never be so proud that we overlook our own weaknesses. Help us to become more aware of the way in which you use them to good advantage.

Showing Discernment

> My son, pay attention to my wisdom; listen carefully to my wise counsel. Then you will show discernment, and your lips will express what you've learned.
> —Proverbs 5:1

"YOU DID WHAT?" we asked the new missionary incredulously.

"I went to the mosque and told them to turn down the volume," he repeated. "The call to prayer over their loudspeakers is far too loud. Just because this country has more Muslims than any other doesn't give them the right to disturb the rest of us."

Here was a missionary who had been sent to work with us because of his maturity and know-how. His age and experience certainly hadn't prevented him from making mistakes. They raised some interesting questions as well.

First, do we as foreign guests have the right to reprimand our hosts or tell them what to do? How would we feel if an Indonesian Muslim did that in Minnesota?

Second, can we assume that the attitudes, beliefs, and values lying beneath the surface of each culture are the same? Airwaves, for example, are public space. In the United States, public space can be used by everyone—but only as long as we don't disturb others in the process. Not so in Indonesia. When our neighbor died, for example, his family set up an awning that went across the public road in front of our house. Traffic was diverted, and chairs were set up on the road to receive mourners. They could use the road because it was public space. The airwaves too are public. A mosque has the right to turn up the volume just as high as it wants. Public space, after all, is public space, they will tell you.

Age and experience can be important assets in making correct judgments. More important yet is the ability to discern. As Solomon taught his son, show discernment, and your lips will express what you've learned. That includes knowing when to speak out and when to keep quiet.

For Reflection

1. Have you ever shown poor judgment and spoken out when you should have held your tongue? What happened?
2. Describe a time when you should have spoken out but kept silent.
3. In your experience, who has helped you the most to become more discerning? What lessons did they teach you?

Source of all wisdom, help us to be respectful and discerning as we encounter new or difficult situations, that our witness as Christians might be effective.

Living Witnesses

> Above all, you must live as citizens of heaven, conducting yourselves in a manner worthy of the Good News about Christ.
> —Philippians 1:27

IT WAS A school holiday—Nag Panchami—the day Hindus throughout India offer milk to snakes to bring prosperity to the family. I was delighted that a Hindu student had invited me to go home with her that day. I was looking forward to meeting her parents and getting to know her better too.

When our rickshaw stopped in front of their house, her parents were standing in the doorway. Pressing their palms together, they greeted me warmly.

"We've met before, you know," her father said.

"We have?" I asked, surprised. "I'm sorry, I'm afraid I don't remember."

"Oh, I don't mean recently," he continued. "It was in a previous incarnation."

I felt totally flustered, and as an inexperienced twenty-two year old, I didn't know what to say. As we went in and sat down, he continued to dominate the conversation. Instead of allowing me to visit with his daughter, he spent the next few hours trying to convert me to Hinduism. As the irritation and anger welled up inside of me, I found it more and more difficult to conduct myself in a manner worthy of the good news.

In my journal that evening I wrote, "If you want to increase your Christian faith, come to India and have Hindus try to convert you. It makes you say the creed and declare to the world, 'Jesus Christ is my Lord and Savior. In Him only do I put my trust.' If India has done anything to me, it has made me a stronger Christian. For that I am most grateful to God!"

Now, many years later, whenever I see Westerners passing out Christian literature in public places or pushing their religion at interfaith events, I think back to that day. I wonder if these well-meaning Christians are having any more luck than my student's father did when he tried to convert me to Hinduism.

For Reflection

1. In what various ways do people witness to their faith?
2. What preconditions should be met before we verbally witness to our faith?
3. What have you found to be the most effective way of witnessing to your faith?

Help us to conduct ourselves in a manner that is worthy of the gospel of Christ, that we may be living witnesses to your eternal light.

In Spite of Us

> But among you it will be different. Whoever wants to be a leader among you must be your servant.
> —Matthew 20:26

PEOPLE STOPPED AND stared as our Indonesian wedding procession passed by. The groom's family had rented a car and two big buses to take us from the groom's house to the ceremony with police escort. As the groom's sponsors, Daniel and I were seated in the car directly behind the lead squad car with its blinking lights and wailing siren.

Our colorful procession wove its way past our university, around a curve, and down a steep hill. Looking back, we were surprised to note that the buses were no longer behind us. How on earth could we have lost them? After waiting for some time, a police officer ran back up the hill to see what had happened. Returning, he chuckled and said, "They've gone a different way." So there we were, the only vehicle in a lost procession, being escorted across town in style by a police car.

When we arrived at our destination, the buses were already there. Asked why they had left the convoy and taken off on their own like that, the drivers explained that it would have been impossible to negotiate the sharp curve and steep hill we had gone down. Instead of getting stuck, they had broken ranks and taken a different route.

Perhaps the lost buses can teach us a lesson in leadership. Many of us who are sent off to assignments in developing countries feel that we know what's best. We try to lead by example. When we look behind us, though, sometimes the "buses" are not coming. Our national partners may not always do what we hope or expect. They know the obstacles along the way better than we do and may feel it is wiser to use a different route to reach the goal. Sometimes they get there, then, not because of us but in spite of us!

For Reflection

1. What are some qualities of effective leaders?
2. Why does a Christian leader need a servant's heart?
3. Why is it necessary for missionaries and other overseas workers to be well-versed in the language and culture of the people they serve?

Give us the wisdom and ability to serve others with humility and grace.

Chapter 6
Confronting Adversity

> Pain is inevitable. Suffering is optional.[10]
> —M. Kathleen Casey

Are You There, God?

> Then call on me when you are in trouble, and I will rescue you, and you will give me glory.
> —Psalm 50:15

MY HUSBAND, DANIEL, grew up in a remote village on the island of Timor in eastern Indonesia. When he was eleven years old, his mother died, leaving six small children. His father remarried and had another five. Then the stepmother became schizophrenic. She beat her children, burned their school books and clothes, and terrified the whole village. His father sold all that he had and did everything he could to find healing for her, but to no avail.

What do you do when there are no facilities for the mentally ill and when the "help me" prayers bring no answers? You try to explain to everyone in the village that this is a sickness, not something the person is doing of his or her free will. You try to put the potential victims out of harm's way. You tie the person to a tree until the violent phase eases—and you submit the problem to God.

Doing that in the 1980s brought us some peace of mind. Now we have just learned that one of the stepmother's sons is showing the very same violent symptoms of schizophrenia.

Life is not fair, and it angers me that one family has to suffer so! If the God I worship is a God of love, why does he appear to be so insensitive? If he is so wonderfully able to help us, why doesn't he do something?

For Reflection

1. My Muslim friend says that when we suffer, God is either punishing us or testing us. Do you agree?
2. What lessons can we learn from the suffering of Christ?
3. What promises of God can help us as we suffer?

When we feel defeated by circumstances beyond our control, help us to remember your promises and turn to you even when we do not feel your guiding presence.

Facing Loss

So Satan left the Lord's presence, and he struck Job with terrible boils from head to foot. Job scraped his skin with a piece of broken pottery as he sat among the ashes. His wife said to him, "Are you still trying to maintain your integrity? Curse God and die." But Job replied, "You talk like a foolish woman. Should we accept only good things from the hand of God and never anything bad?"
—Job 2:7-10

ONE MORNING WHEN my husband and I were on campus, his sister phoned us. She sounded urgent. "When are you coming home?" she asked. "I think someone has broken into the house."

Surely not, I thought, heading for home. Like most property in Java, our land was encircled by a high wall that protected it. Our part-time gardener would have been working outside, and we had three dogs who would bark if a thief were to break in. My sister-in-law was right, though. Our upstairs screen window had been slit, and all of the drawers in our dressers had been pulled out. The door to our locked built-in cabinets had been pried open as well.

We were shocked when we assessed the damage. The thief had stolen my husband's laptop and new digital camera, jewelry, watches, family heirlooms, and farewell gifts from my students. Even my mother's diamond engagement ring was missing. How could this have happened, we kept asking ourselves as the police dusted for fingerprints. It was a great loss to us since nothing had been insured. What had we done to deserve this fate?

What had Job done to deserve his fate? What did the prophets and apostles do to deserve plagues, famines, beatings, and prison? Jesus had suffered an even worse fate. Why should we expect anything less? In the words of Job, "Should we accept only good things from the hand of God and never anything bad?"

For Reflection

1. Why does God allow bad things to happen to us?
2. How does God want us to face the problems we encounter in life?
3. What doesn't kill you makes you stronger, it is said. In what way have hardships in your own life helped you to grow stronger?

May we face hardships with courage, realizing that we do not walk alone and that you will help to see us through.

The Test of Courage

> Bless those who persecute you. Don't curse them; pray that God will bless them.
> —Romans 12:14

SINCE 9/11, THE challenge to live out our Christian calling around the world has become increasingly difficult. To be reviled and hated, even by a few extremists, creates fear. To be in the minority in such a situation takes courage. What is the church to do in countries like Indonesia when extremists like Abu Bakar Ba'asyir claim, "Between you and us there will forever be a ravine of hate, and we will be enemies until you follow Allah's law."[11]? When the police arrest religious militants and discover maps of our campus and a plot to bomb our university, we know the threat is real.

How should we, who worship a God of love, present ourselves in such a situation? We agonize over what the Christian minority should do to bridge this ravine of hate. Some say we should build walls to separate ourselves from the majority. Others recommend fighting fire with fire.

Before we do anything, obviously we need to study the situation carefully to learn how many support the claim of extremists and how fast this ravine of hate is growing. We need to reflect upon the past and learn causes. We need to learn what we have done to warrant such hate. Only then can we seek just solutions.

To be in the minority in such a situation takes courage. It takes courage to be wise and to heed that gentle voice that exhorts us to clothe ourselves with compassion, kindness, humility, meekness, and patience. As Tekmito Adegemo so shrewdly put it, "We cannot preach good news and be bad news."[12]

For Reflection

1. Have you ever been in a situation where it took courage to be in the minority? How did you manage?
2. In what ways does persecution strengthen the church?
3. In what specific ways should we bless those who persecute us?

Give us the wisdom and strength we need to represent Christ to the world, even when we are in the minority.

When Disaster Strikes

> My God, my God, why have you abandoned me? Why are you so far away when I groan for help?
> —Psalm 22:1

IN DECEMBER 2004, friends of ours from Aceh, North Sumatra, flew to Saudi Arabia to join the annual pilgrimage to Mecca. While they were gone, their relatives gathered at their home by the sea to celebrate an important birthday of a family member. What a joyous occasion for them all!

Early the next morning, however, an immense earthquake struck off the west coast of Sumatra, and the ground began shaking violently. When the tremors ceased, everyone ran outside to discover that the ocean waters had receded. Hundreds of fish were flopping on the dry sand, so neighbors in all directions came running to help gather up the fish. Suddenly one of the men looked up and screamed, "Run!" An immense black wall of water was rushing toward them. They turned and ran for their lives. Some lived to tell the tale, but most did not.

By the time our friends returned from Mecca, Aceh had been turned into a wasteland. In despair, the couple tried to figure out where their house had been located. Nothing was left, of course, and worse yet, their children, parents, and close relatives had all been washed out to sea and drowned. Not one survived. The couple was not alone in their grief, however. This devastating tsunami had killed nearly 230,000 people in eleven countries.

"Why?" we ask as we struggle to find answers.

For Reflection

1. What natural disasters have you experienced firsthand? What was your reaction?
2. Has a natural disaster ever shaken your faith in God?
3. What valuable lessons have natural disasters taught you?

When disaster strikes, oh God of mercy, calm our anxious hearts and assure us that you have not forsaken us but are standing beside us as our refuge and strength.

When the Earth Shook

> God is our refuge and strength, always ready to help in times of trouble. So we will not fear when earthquakes come and the mountains crumble into the sea.
> —Psalm 46:1-2

A UNIVERSITY COLLEAGUE of ours, whom I will call Maria, is married to a pastor in Yogyakarta. Every weekend she makes the two-hour trip home to spend time with her family. That weekend in 2006 was no exception.

When Maria and her husband were driving out of Yogyakarta to visit relatives that Saturday, they wondered what on earth had come over them. Suddenly, the trees along the side of the road began waving violently, and cars started careening across the highway. Every motorcycle in front of their car toppled over, throwing drivers and passengers across the pavement. Their own car was shaking so intensely that they could barely control it. They held on and were finally able to pull off to the side of the road.

The road on which they had been traveling was lined with houses on both sides. When the shaking stopped, every single house in sight collapsed to the ground like a deck of cards. Maria and her husband sat in their car amid a sea of rubble and dust, too stunned for words. They were dazed but unharmed.

When the dust settled, the couple made a U-turn and headed back home. Upon reaching their street, they were astounded to find that only their church and parsonage were still standing. Every other house had been flattened, crushing many of the owners inside.

That weekend Maria and her husband became a blessing to many. They turned their battered church and parsonage into centers of refuge for those in the neighborhood who had survived the earthquake.

For Reflection

1. What reliable Christian relief agencies are known internationally for assisting survivors after a natural disaster?
2. What kinds of problems have well-meaning church groups encountered or caused while carrying out relief work independently in another culture?
3. Is it ethical to use the tragedy of a natural disaster as an opportunity to evangelize while distributing aid? Why or why not?

When disasters strike, help us to become wise sources of comfort, blessing, and refuge to those in need.

Modern Day Miracle

> Even though the fig trees have no blossoms, and there are no grapes on the vines; even though the olive crop fails, and the fields lie empty and barren; even though the flocks die in the fields, and the cattle barns are empty, yet I will rejoice in the Lord! I will be joyful in the God of my salvation!
> —Habakkuk 3:17-18

A JAVANESE FRIEND of ours lives in Yogyakarta but works in Semarang, three hours away. He drives home from work on Friday evenings and drives back again to Semarang on Sunday.

One Friday night he drove to Yogyakarta for the weekend as usual. The next morning, however, for some reason he had the strongest urge to turn right around and drive back to his place of work in Semarang. Why, he wasn't quite sure, but the urge was so strong that he followed his instincts.

When he told the family that he was leaving, they were stunned. Why did he have to take off so suddenly and why so early in the morning? Couldn't he at least wait until after lunch to leave? Insisting that he had to go, he walked outside and got

102 Light for the Journey

into the car parked in front of the house. His wife and children all followed and gathered around the car to say good-bye. Suddenly they felt the earth shake and heard a loud roar. They were shocked to see their house collapse to the ground in back of them. All of them had been saved from the earthquake that struck that May 27th morning because they happened to be outside saying good-bye at the time....saved because of the father's mysterious urge to leave so early that morning.

The family was overwhelmed with gratitude to be alive. Instead of grieving for the loss of their home and possessions, they called their relatives and friends to a special thanksgiving service to praise God for his care and protection.

For Reflection

1. Have you ever experienced a miraculous escape? How did you respond afterwards?
2. Recall a bad situation that brought good to your life.

3. When something bad happens, why is it better to praise God instead of complaining?

No matter what happens in my life, may I rejoice and speak of your glory and grace!

Hope for a New Day

~~~

> We are pressed on every side by troubles, but we are not crushed. We are perplexed, but not driven to despair. We are hunted down, but never abandoned by God. We get knocked down, but we are not destroyed.
> —2 Corinthians 4:8-9

OUR HOUSE SHUDDERED and creaked as the earth rumbled. Alarmed, we scurried down the stairs and out into the yard.

A volcanic eruption would have lasted longer than that, we surmised. It must have been an earthquake. Little did we realize that at that very moment houses and buildings just sixty miles south of us were collapsing, pinning thousands of innocent victims under the weight of wood, cement, and concrete. Over 6,000 people died in the earthquake.

Reputable relief agencies sprang into action. Indonesians too helped each other, donating food and clothes to those who had lost everything. Women gathered to cook in neighborhood kitchens, providing one home-cooked meal a day for the needy in their area.

Hope for a New Day *105*

Students from our Christian university stood at the traffic lights with donation boxes for earthquake relief. They also collected over $100 a day in small change from people entering the campus. The university sent truckloads of student volunteers to help clear out the rubble, and doctors from our polyclinic to assist those who had not yet received the help they needed. Tuition fees were dropped for students from earthquake survivor families.

Little by little, despair was replaced by hope.

For Reflection

1. What causes you to lose hope?
2. From what sources do you normally seek hope when you need it?
3. Think of a time when someone shared his or her feelings of hopelessness with you. What did you do? What could you have done better?

Help us to be resilient and to remember that there is always hope for a new day, for you are always with us.

Chapter 7

Facing Fear

Fear can keep us up all night long,
But faith makes one fine pillow.[13]
—Philip Gulley

Things That Go Bump in the Night

This is my command—be strong and courageous! Do not be afraid or discouraged. For the Lord your God is with you wherever you go.
—Joshua 1:9

"AREN'T YOU AFRAID to work in your office after dark?" the library department heads asked me at our weekly meeting.

"Why?" I asked. "A campus security officer is always around."

"But you have to go up the stairs to your balcony office!" they exclaimed. "The ghost who lives under the stairs with her children comes out at night."

When I became the director of a Christian university library in Central Java, I never expected to spend so much staff meeting time talking about ghosts. Just the other night a cleaner had reportedly seen the woman and her children, but that wasn't all. The head of technical services had run into a headless man on the stairs, and even a campus security officer had warned that the library was haunted. Why on earth had the library been built within sight of the cemetery just across the campus wall, anyway?

Because I had never experienced the supernatural, ghosts did not seem real to me and therefore did not frighten me. The trepidation my staff felt, however, was certainly real, and their fear was contagious. Even though they acknowledged that God would never abandon them and that Jesus was stronger than any evil spirit, they kept on worrying. Inevitably we would have to stop the meeting and bow our heads in prayer until God had calmed their fears.

For Reflection

1. What stories of demons and evil spirits are mentioned in the Bible? What do you make of them?
2. Have you ever had an experience that convinced you that ghosts and evil spirits are real in today's world?
3. How can we help others to face and overcome their fears?

Merciful Father, help us to be compassionate toward those who experience fear, particularly those who fear what we do not. Help us to trust that you are greater than all our fears.

God's Peace

> I am leaving you with a gift—peace of mind and heart. And the gift I give is a gift the world cannot give. So don't be troubled or afraid.
>
> —John 14:27

WHAT DO YOU do when you are troubled or afraid about the future? Friends of mine in Hong Kong often turn to fortune-tellers and spiritualists at such times. They consult astrologers to determine the luckiest day for opening a new business, taking off on a long journey, or celebrating a wedding. They also travel long distances to the graves of important people to pray for health, success, or sudden wealth.

Many Indonesians consult paranormals when they feel intimidated or that something bad has happened. For example, when the night watchman at our Christian university felt threatened by the ghosts residing in our library, he called in a shaman to placate the ghosts. When a missionary colleague at the Faculty of Theology had his laptop stolen from a locked filing cabinet in his office, a campus security officer called in a psychic who could reportedly discover the identity of the thief through a special piece of bamboo placed at the back of the filing cabinet. When our house was robbed, a Javanese neighbor consulted an out-of-town mystic to find out what the thieves looked like.

These are not animists or cult members seeking the help of spiritualists but ordinary Christians like you and me. It should not surprise us, for many in our own culture do the same thing. When anxious or worried, they call psychic hotlines or visit psychic fairs to have clairvoyants or mediums perform readings, interpret dreams, lift curses, and communicate with the dead.

When we are troubled or afraid, do we find the peace of mind we are seeking from our faith, or do we prefer to depend upon that "fragile peace" which the world gives?

For Reflection

1. What do you do to restore a sense of peace when worries or fears besiege you?
2. Is there anything wrong in seeking advice from a paranormal or spiritualist at such times? Why or why not?
3. How might focusing on God's promises help to bring us peace?

As we face problems and challenges, may we respond from the Spirit within us which empowers us, guides us, and gives us that peace which the world cannot give.

Calming the Storm Within Us

> Then he asked them, "Why are you afraid? Do you still have no faith?"
>
> —Mark 4:40

DANIEL'S UNCLE MICHAEL was swimming for his life that night, desperately trying to survive in a stormy sea. Hours earlier, his sailboat had capsized in the treacherous straits between Timor and Rote in eastern Indonesia. Exhausted and weakened from struggling in the water for hours, he began to sense that death was near.

Few of us have experienced the kind of perils Michael did that night, but all of us have faced tough situations in life. Death takes away a loved one, a thief breaks in and steals our prized possessions, our house is foreclosed in a housing crisis, or an unexpected recession wipes away our life's savings.

How do we react when the storms of life overturn our boats? Do we lose heart? Do we ask God, "Don't you care that this is happening to me?" just as the disciples did before Jesus calmed the storm on the Sea of Galilee? Would Jesus turn to us too and ask, "Why are you afraid? Do you still have no faith?" Could it be that God has not withdrawn from us, but that our faith has weakened in the face of trial?

Sometimes miracles do happen, as Michael experienced that night in the choppy sea. As he struggled to keep afloat, he felt a nudge. There it was again! Under the water something was lifting him and pushing him along, propelling him towards a distant shore. Only after he reached land did he realize what had saved his life. A dolphin had seen him struggling and had befriended him in the high seas, pushing him to shore. Today Michael's children, nephews, and nieces continue to tell his amazing story, just as my husband Daniel told it to me.

God does not always create a miracle like he did for Michael. He does, however, still the storms of fear and anxiety in our hearts. He does enable us to face life with courage if only we have faith.

For Reflection

1. Describe a time when you felt let down or totally abandoned by God.
2. Has God ever revealed himself to you or a family member in a miraculous way?
3. How do we maintain or restore our faith in God when we are engulfed by the storms of life?

Empower us with the courage, strength, and faith we need to withstand the trials that come our way.

Panic in Jerusalem

In panic I cried out, "I am cut off from the Lord!" But you heard my cry for mercy and answered my call for help.
—Psalm 31:22

I WAS GRIPPED by fear. Two rough-looking men had sneaked up behind me and had suddenly linked their arms in mine.

"Pretend nothing is happening," whispered the young man on my right. "You are coming with us to the King David Hotel!"

Oh, God! I thought in panic. A few minutes before that, a service car from Ramallah had dropped me off at the Damascus Gate in Jerusalem. I had assured my Palestinian colleague that I would be just fine walking alone up to the guesthouse where I stayed during the weekends. After all, it was only a three-block walk. And now…

"Get your hands off of me!" I barked, struggling to set myself free.

As I scuffled with the two men, the voice of an angel called out, "Rosella, are you in trouble?"

Stunned, the men released me and fled.

Who had called my name? As I looked up, astonished, it was not an angel I saw but a woman standing on the corner. She had been waiting for the bus there when she saw me trying to fight the two men off.

"You've got to be careful!" she admonished as I came closer. What a surprise! It was the wife of the bishop who lived at the guesthouse where I was staying. I had met her at supper the previous weekend, and afterwards she had invited me up to their apartment to listen to the BBC news on their shortwave radio. Little did I realize then what a lifeline she would prove to be for me.

For Reflection

1. What experience in your life has made you realize that God works in mysterious ways?
2. What is the most frightening situation you have ever encountered? Did you feel God's presence at the time, or did you feel abandoned by God?
3. How can you help others to see God's provision in times of trouble?

Guide us, direct us, and protect us each day, oh Lord, as we journey through the perils of life.

A Living Nightmare

As Pharaoh approached, the people of Israel looked up and panicked when they saw the Egyptians overtaking them. They cried out to the Lord.
—Exodus 14:10

WHEN OUR DOG in North Sumatra bit the woman who delivered eggs, we were shocked at his behavior. This just wasn't like him. A fellow missionary told us to muzzle the dog and keep him under observation for two weeks. This we did, although it seemed silly at the time. After all, the dog had recently been vaccinated against rabies, and we had the papers to prove it.

When our dog worked his muzzle off the next week and bit a neighbor lady, we knew we were in for trouble. We began keeping him tied when he was outdoors and only allowed him to be free indoors.

The next week, as I was finishing up a language lesson with my Batak tutor, the dog suddenly attacked her, biting her feet and legs. We both screamed and managed to lock the dog in the kitchen. Even though I didn't have a driver's license and had never driven in North Sumatra before, I grabbed the mission car keys and rushed my tutor to the hospital to be stitched up. Then we contacted the vet. She told us to bring the dog to her office the next morning.

Later that evening another missionary came over to visit. Our dog greeted him joyfully and then turned on the man in rage. The three of us raced for my room and slammed the door. Terrified, we sat on the edge of my bed, paralyzed by fear, not knowing what to do.

What did the Israelites do, trapped between the Egyptians and the sea? Time and again God had provided for them. We had to trust that He would do the same for us.

For Reflection

1. How do you normally react when you are confronted with a sudden crisis?
2. What helps you to face crises courageously?
3. It is said that hardships help you to grow. What Bible verses would substantiate this?

Help us to remember that even in the face of danger you are with us as our refuge and strength.

Chapter 8
Doing What's Right

We cannot preach good news and be bad news.[14]
—Tekmito Adegemo

The Importance of Integrity

> People with integrity walk safely, but those who follow crooked paths will slip and fall.
> —Proverbs 10:9

WHEN THE VET came to take our dog away the day after he attacked our friends, our entire household in North Sumatra was deeply troubled. We were quite sure that he had somehow contracted rabies. We were worried about our friends who had been bitten, and we were saddened that our dog had suffered so unnecessarily. He died the next day. To determine whether rabies had been the cause of death, one of us had to take his brain in a cooler to neighboring Singapore.

A week later we learned that our dog had tested positive for rabies. How could this have happened? We had been diligent about getting his full series of shots each year and had had him vaccinated against rabies. In fact, the dog had just been vaccinated a few months before that, and we had the papers to prove it.

In a country where corruption runs rampant, uncovering causes can be difficult if not impossible. Had the anti-rabies vaccine been contaminated somewhere down the line? We would never know. Had the veterinarian substituted something else for the costly vaccine and pocketed the difference at our expense? We would never know. Who was to blame? We would never know. All we knew was that someone else's mistake or lack of integrity had caused a great deal of pain and suffering. Someone else's slipup or dishonesty had also burned a hole in our pockets. We wound up paying for everything, from the victims' emergency medical treatment to the series of fourteen painful injections for six of us.

How hard it is to uphold high ethical standards when we can so easily excuse our crooked paths and lack of integrity by saying, "So what? Everybody's doing it." As Voltaire once noted, "No snowflake in an avalanche ever feels responsible."[15]

For Reflection

1. Which stories in the Bible come to mind when you think of the word "integrity"?
2. Which kinds of situations test your own moral fiber the most?
3. In what specific ways can you become an example of moral and ethical strength in your own home and place of work?

May the knowledge that you are walking by our side keep us on the straight path of integrity, oh Lord.

Save the Children

> And anyone who welcomes a little child like this on my behalf is welcoming me.
> —Matthew 18:5

WHILE LIVING IN Australia, we learned a good deal about indigenous Australians who, like the American Indians, were herded onto reserves or missions in the early 1800s. How their children suffered! Known as the "stolen generation," from 1885 until 1969 these aboriginal children were separated from their parents and forced to work for white families. Australian friends of ours often justified the policy by pointing out that the children had actually been offered a better way of life. Only in 2008 did Australia officially apologize to the aboriginal community for laws and policies that had affronted their dignity and caused them such loss.

We needn't point fingers at the Australians when it comes to "saving the children," though, for well-meaning Christians around the world are often just as guilty. What did an Idaho church group do when Haiti was devastated by an earthquake in 2010? They rounded up all the stray children they could find and tried to take them out of Haiti to give them a better life—even though one-third of the children had parents who had survived the quake. Their busload of children was stopped at the Dominican Republic border and the perpetrators arrested. Nations are responsible for protecting their own citizens, after all, and they have the right and obligation to prevent the trafficking of their children.

Our hearts go out to children caught up in devastating situations, and we yearn to help. When children were orphaned by the 2004 tsunami, people from Indonesia and around the world offered to adopt them. When Indonesia's first lady visited devastated Aceh, she too suggested that she could adopt a few of the children. Interestingly enough, the children politely refused her offer, saying that they preferred to stay on in Aceh. Indeed, this is the least traumatic solution for children. We give them the best gift of all when we not only allow but help them to remain within their own culture and community.

For Reflection

1. Was it necessary for Australia to offer an apology to its aboriginal people for the way they were treated by previous generations? Why or why not?
2. What other apologies should be offered to children of our world today?
3. How has your church or community helped children displaced by wars or natural disasters? What ethical issues have they faced in their work?

Stretch out your loving arms, oh Lord, to enfold children traumatized or orphaned by wars or natural disasters. Teach us how best to serve them for your name's sake.

Digging Out the Roots

> Anyone who continues to live in him will not sin. But anyone who keeps on sinning does not know him or understand who he is.
>
> —1 John 3:6

WHEN MY INDONESIAN husband and I bought a piece of land in Central Java and were preparing to build a house, we discussed landscaping options. Bamboo has such a delicate look about it and has always been a favorite of mine. I suggested we plant some in our courtyard.

"You don't know much about bamboo, do you!" my husband said, laughing. "The sectioned stalks and slender leaves of bamboo are lovely to

look at," he explained, "but if you plant bamboo, nothing else will be able to grow. The bamboo roots will spread underground and choke out everything else. If you decide to cut the bamboo down later on, it will just grow back, because the roots are still there."

Temptation and sin are like that, aren't they? The longer we continue accepting bribes, cheating on our spouses, or telling lies, the easier it becomes. The more we become addicted to it, the more harmless it seems. It becomes harder and harder to stop, for the habit spreads just like the roots of the bamboo tree. Until we dig out the roots in the vulnerable places of our lives and replace them with good soil, we continue to sin.

It is one thing to make a mistake but quite another to continue to make the same mistake. Resisting temptation and breaking the cycle becomes easier as we invite Christ to take root in our lives and transform us.

For Reflection

1. What is your greatest weakness at this stage in your life? What temptations attract you most?
2. What practical things can you do to resist those temptations?
3. When sin gets the best of you and you hurt yourself or others, what helps you to make things right and to get your life back on track?

Help us to fill the vulnerable places of our lives with good soil that we might become more like Christ in thought, word, and deed.

A Knock at the Door

For I recognize my rebellion; it haunts me day and night.
—Psalm 51:3

THE STUDENT SITTING in the back row of Daniel's public policy class seemed particularly unfriendly. Like many graduate students in development studies at Satya Wacana Christian University, he was an Indonesian government official. He was also a leader in one of the nation's largest Muslim organizations.

As the weeks went by, his bitterness continued; he made cynical remarks and openly challenged his professor at every chance he could get. Even though Daniel became more and more annoyed as the semester went on, he decided that becoming angry at this arrogant student would only make things worse. Instead, he held his temper and always responded politely. In time, the student finished his degree and left the university.

One day several semesters later, Daniel's thoughts were interrupted by a knock at his office door. There stood the antagonistic government official. He asked if he could come in and then sat down across from Daniel.

"I have come to apologize," he said.

Examining his hands as he talked, he admitted that his behavior in class had been entirely inappropriate. He explained that he had come to study at Satya Wacana even though he disliked Christians, because he knew it was the best place to get a degree in development studies. As time went on, however, he had mellowed because the Christians around him were not hostile toward him but peaceful and reconciling.

The Muslim official's opinion of Christians had changed dramatically because of the way those around him had conducted themselves. Never underestimate the difference our behavior as Christians makes in the eyes of others!

For Reflection

1. Have you ever had someone come and apologize to you for his or her behavior? How did the apology affect your relationship with that person?
2. What do you specifically need to apologize for to a parent, spouse, or child?
3. In what way has your own behavior witnessed to your faith?

Make us mindful of how others are affected by what we say and do. When relationships are strained or broken, help us to knock on the door and seek to restore them.

Of Dogs and Footwear

> Getting wisdom is the wisest thing you can do! And whatever else you do, develop good judgment.
> —Proverbs 4:7

IN NORTH SUMATRA, our mission driver was a Muslim from the island of Java. Sahar only had a sixth-grade education, but he loved to theorize. One day when he was driving me to Medan to buy books for our library, he turned and exclaimed, "Rosie, I could never become a Christian!"

What prompted him to start debating religion in the car that morning, I have no idea, but his statement intrigued me. "Why is that?" I asked out of curiosity. "Why could you never become a Christian?"

"Because Christians eat dogs, that's why!" he asserted, as though I were overlooking the obvious.

Well, he had a point there. You see, dog meat is a delicacy among the Batak people of North Sumatra. Most Bataks are Christians, and since Bataks eat dogs, obviously Christians eat dogs.

We may laugh at Sahar for using such twisted logic, but how many well-meaning, educated Western Christians do the very same thing?

When I was visiting Minnesota recently, for example, a friend from church asked me, "Rosie, is our President a Muslim?"

I refrained from asking what difference that would make and asked instead what made her think he might be a Muslim. Her response showed how little she knew about Islam.

"Well," she said, "he took off his shoes to go into a mosque just like Muslims do, and surely that says something."

"But does he change his clothes, roll down a prayer mat, face Mecca, and prostate himself five times a day in prayer?" I asked. "Does he read the Qur'an in Arabic and go to the mosque on Fridays at eleven o'clock? Does he avoid pork and alcohol? Does he fast from morning till night during Ramadan, the fasting month? Has he made the required trip to Mecca?"

Indeed, if removing his shoes before entering a mosque made our President a Muslim, I told her, then I must be a Muslim too.

For Reflection

1. What half-truths are contained in the two incidents described above?
2. Why are half-truths so deceptive? Why do we fall for them more easily than plain lies and falsehoods?
3. How should we respond when we receive forwarded stories or rumors with half-truths aimed at spreading fear or hatred?

Teach us to be discerning about the truth, O Lord. Help us to develop good judgment and guard against the temptation of using deceptive means to advance our own religious or political convictions or agendas.

Wise Choices

> Wise choices will watch over you. Understanding will keep you safe.
> —Proverbs 2:11

AFTER SERVING AS an educational missionary in North Sumatra for three years, I was asked to move down an island for a year to take the place of a missionary who had been teaching at Satya Wacana Christian University in Central Java. That was the year that changed my life. When it came time to leave, I discovered that I was not only leaving a place I had grown to love but an Indonesian man I had become very attached to as well.

At the end of my term in Central Java, I returned to the United States to begin a year-long Indonesian studies program, sponsored by the Lutheran Church in America. I found it increasingly difficult to concentrate on my studies without Daniel, even though letters helped to bridge the world that separated us. It was no surprise to me when he proposed several months later. I was excited about our future prospects, feeling that I could carry out my missionary work in Indonesia more effectively with new vision and insight if I were married to a national.

The joy that Daniel and I felt, however, was soon tempered by the misgivings of my church's program director. It was not that he disliked Daniel or worried that our cross-cultural marriage would fail. It was simply that our church would not allow it. In the 1970s, male missionaries were permitted to marry foreign nationals, but female missionaries were not. That was the rule.

What was I to do? If I married Daniel, I would lose my job with my church. If I didn't marry him, I would lose my mind. The Bible encourages us to choose the right path. Sometimes, however, the right choice isn't all that obvious.

For Reflection

1. What are some of the points we need to consider when facing difficult decisions?
2. Think back on a time when you had a hard choice to make. How did you figure out what to do?
3. Is the church more inclusive now than it used to be in the 1970s? In what ways is it still exclusive?

When we are faced with painful decisions, help us to make choices that are wise.

Chapter 9
Giving and Receiving

For it is in giving that we receive.[16]
—St. Francis of Assisi

Filling the Baskets

> Whatever you give is acceptable if you give it eagerly. And give according to what you have, not what you don't have.
> —2 Corinthians 8:12

IN MY HUSBAND'S Timorese culture, when someone gives us a basket of bananas or avocados from the garden, we never return the basket empty. Whether it is oranges or homemade candy, we always find something of our own to put inside before we return it. As we receive, so we give.

Is this not what God is asking of us too? Through Christ's death and resurrection, God has restored a right relationship with us. He has given us his Son that we might live life abundantly. He has filled us with good things. How will we fill these empty baskets to return the favor to him?

We can return the favor by using the talents God has given us, remembering that much is required from those to whom much has been given. We should be on the lookout for opportunities to use our understanding, our resources, and our abilities.

One of the best ways we can fill those baskets is with the gift of companionship and a generous heart. As Virginia Satir, noted American author and psychotherapist, has said, "How often have I noticed people who looked without seeing, listened without hearing, spoke without meaning, moved without awareness, touched without feeling... The greatest gift I can give is to see, hear, understand, and to touch another person."[17]

For Reflection

1. What special talents, aptitudes, and abilities do you have? List them.
2. In what ways are you currently developing and using those talents to the glory of God?
3. Describe a time when someone gave you the gift of companionship and a generous heart just at a time when you needed it most.

In thanks for the gift of life and the gift of your Son, may we strive to reach out and give of ourselves.

Corn and Beans

Since God chose you to be the holy people he loves, you must clothe yourselves with tenderhearted mercy, kindness, humility, gentleness and patience.
—Colossians 3:12

TWO OF OUR most important American cultural values are individualism and independence. Those who move to another culture, however, soon come to understand that these American values are by no means universal. When I married an Indonesian, I discovered that the extended family did not value individualism and independence but cooperation and mutual support.

All members of the extended family are expected to know who they are in relation to the others and where their responsibilities lie. As the eldest member of our family and a university lecturer, my husband was expected to provide his brothers and sisters with an education. And so it was that four of my husband's brothers, sisters, and cousins came from West Timor to live with us. We paid their way to Java, and we paid their tuition. They in turn took care of the house and cooked the meals. Our son grew up surrounded by aunts and uncles, and we never had to look for a babysitter.

The relationship within our Indonesian extended family is somewhat like the relationship that corn and green beans enjoy in a Timorese garden. Corn and green beans are planted in the same hole. As the corn stalk grows, it provides a pole for the beans to climb. The beans, in turn, replenish the soil with nutrients to help the corn grow. Ideally the extended family offers that kind of mutual solidarity and support, and expects loyalty in return. It provides the good soil in which mercy, kindness, humility, gentleness, and patience can grow.

For Reflection

1. What similarities do you see between the relationship corn and beans enjoy and the bond we enjoy with God as he relates to us personally?
2. In what ways do your own family members support and nourish each other?

3. In what ways can we who are planted in the same cultural hole remain individualistic and independent, yet work together for the common good?

Heavenly Father, help us to serve you loyally by respecting your creation and extending the love we have received from you to others.

For Just Such a Time as This

> A friend is always loyal, and a brother is born to help in time of need.
> —Proverbs 17:17

AT ITS BEST, there is a gracious give and take to the way Timorese extended family members bear one another's burdens. Relatives are there for each other, especially in time of need.

Years ago when my husband was completing his degree at Satya Wacana Christian University in Central Java, he went home to the island of Timor to do research on the cattle trade there. When it came time for him to return to the university, he discovered that he did not have enough money to pay for the three-day boat trip back to Java. What was he to do?

Hearing of his plight, his Uncle Nitanil walked from the remote village of Taloi for two days to Daniel's village, pulling a cow behind him. When he got there, he sold the cow to pay for Daniel's ticket back to Java. The cow was there, he said, for just such a time as this.

A good turn is never forgotten. Nitanil's own son is now living with us in Central Java as we put him through the university.

The extended family system has its weaknesses, but it can teach us something too. As brothers and sisters in Christ, we should be there for one another. Are we? What do we need to do to make our homes and churches stronger centers of mutual support, especially in time of need?

For Reflection

1. In what ways has your own family helped you in times of need?
2. In what ways could you better contribute to the welfare of your relatives?
3. What sacrifices have you made in helping others?

May we have gracious hearts, oh God, to see the needs of others and carry one another's burdens.

Sharing Burdens

Share each other's burdens, and in this way obey the law of Christ.
—Galatians 6:2

AT THE CHRISTIAN school in India where I was teaching, a Hindu student once told me, "We should always feel privileged to help a Brahmin."

When I asked why, she said, "When you help a Brahmin, you are helping someone in whom God dwells more fully than in a person of any other caste."

"OK," I responded. "I can understand what you are saying, but how different from my religion! For Christians, we are all important—every single one of us. It is a privilege to help anyone because all people are of the same caste—the very highest caste. God dwells equally in us all."

Even though I knew in my heart that we don't always feel privileged to help the people around us, I knew we should. Paul reminds us too that we should be especially mindful of other Christians because we share a special relationship with those in Christ.

I thought of this when, at one of our mission meetings, a young American remarked, "I've been feeling down and very lonely this entire year."

The oldest member of our group looked at her sadly, shaking his head. "If you are lonely and frustrated, then somehow I have failed," he said.

His point is worth noting. If we are to obey our Lord's command and share one another's burdens, should we not feel personally responsible when another person, especially another Christian, is feeling lonely or defeated? Should we not feel privileged to help?

For Reflection

1. When was the last time you felt genuine compassion for someone who was feeling defeated? What did you do to share that person's burdens?
2. How can we learn to be more sensitive to the needs of others?
3. Recall a time when people showed compassion or helped you through a difficult patch. Which acts of kindness did you appreciate and which did you not?

Open our eyes to the needs of others, oh God of mercy. Remind us that all people are important, and help us to minister to them and share their burdens.

The Gift of Listening

> Understand this, my dear brothers and sisters: You must all be quick to listen, slow to speak, and slow to get angry.
> —James 1:19

WHEN OUR SON was small, a Javanese housekeeper of ours had seemed preoccupied and deeply disturbed for days on end. She began coming in so late that she barely had time to do the chores, and her daughter kept phoning her at odd times during the day. She looked drawn and haggard.

Finally, Daniel called her into our office. "For some time now you have not been yourself," he told her. "If you have a problem, please sit down and tell us about it."

A flood of words and tears burst forth as this employee of ours related all of the troubles her family had been experiencing. Her daughter's husband had run off with another woman. As if that weren't bad enough, the other woman was terrorizing the daughter with nasty phone calls and using black magic to torment her.

There was so much we wanted to say. When we ourselves had never believed in black magic, though, how could we possibly understand the situation or advise her without sounding judgmental? We would gladly have sent her to a trained counselor or psychotherapist if only one had been available in our area at the time. As it was, we could do nothing but sit quietly and simply listen.

The next day our housekeeper thanked us profusely for asking about her problems and taking them seriously. She said that just having had the chance to talk about her problems with someone who truly cared enough to listen had lightened her burden. For that she was so very grateful.

Active listening is not something that comes easy for most of us, but we need to practice it as often as we can. After all, as Paul Tillich reminds us, "The first duty of love is to listen."[18]

For Reflection

1. When was the last time you helped a friend simply by listening?
2. What are some of the things that prevent us from becoming good listeners?
3. What qualities do you look for in a friend with whom you would share your suffering?

May we become increasingly sensitive to the needs of others, oh Lord, and lighten their burdens by listening compassionately with our ears, minds, and hearts.

A Perfect Stranger

꧁꧂

> For I was hungry, and you fed me. I was thirsty, and you gave me a drink. I was a stranger, and you invited me into your home.
> —Matthew 25:35

MY PLANE TOUCHED down in Vienna in the middle of a rainstorm that cold October night. Suffering from a head cold and jetlag, I felt miserable and could hardly wait to get to bed.

I had booked a room at a small hotel in the city, so I caught a cab and was soon on my way through the torrents of rain. Finally, the taxi stopped in front of an old, poorly lit building. Could this be the hotel I had ordered? The driver assured me it was as I counted out foreign coins to pay him. Exhausted, I dragged my two suitcases up three flights of winding stone stairs to the reception desk on the third floor.

When I gave the desk clerk my name, she checked her list and then slowly began shaking her head. *"Noooo,"* she said. "No reservation under that name."

"Are you sure?" I asked, certain that she had made a mistake. "I ordered the room two weeks ago."

"Yes, I'm sure," she replied, "and we're fully booked."

What was I to do? There I was, dead tired in a foreign country in the middle of the night with no place to stay. The desk clerk handed me the phone and helped me call several other hotels in the vicinity, but every hotel was full. My heart sank.

Indeed, everything seems harder to bear when we are in a new culture without the benefit of the language. Feeling bewildered and frightened, my eyes welled up with tears. "You're OK. Don't panic!" I kept telling myself, praying for God's guidance.

As I stood there feeling tired, lost, and dejected, a cleaning lady mopping the floor nearby stopped and turned to me. "Excuse me, but I couldn't help overhearing," she whispered in a thick brogue. "Why don't you come home with me for the night? I have an extra room where you could stay."

And so that night I went home with Mrs. Sobena, a cleaning lady who had come to my rescue and invited me in. Decades have passed since then, but I remember her still, for when I was a stranger, she invited me into her home.

For Reflection

1. What is the kindest thing a stranger has ever done for you?
2. What is the kindest thing you have ever done for a stranger?
3. Who are the strangers in your own community, and what can you do to make them feel more at home?

Help us to become more sensitive toward the needs of strangers and to meet those needs as we are able.

By Our Love

Love your neighbor as yourself.
—Leviticus 19:18

AS OUR BUS pulled into the station in Srinagar, Kashmir, my friend Anne and I felt puzzled. How would we ever recognize Noor, the man from whom we were to rent a small houseboat for a month? And then we saw him, smiling shyly, holding up the letter we had sent. After greeting us warmly, Noor escorted us along Chinar Bagh to a plain, unpainted wooden D-class houseboat. Next to it was a larger B-class boat and Noor's own boat, which housed eleven relatives in six tiny bare wooden rooms.

It was early May, and we were freezing. To help us keep warm, Noor brought us blankets, hot tea, and a crockery-lined basket of hot coals. During the day, his wife would graciously serve us hot, home-cooked meals in the larger B-class boat even though we were only paying for D-class facilities. In the evening, Noor would come to our boat to listen to the small radio he had put there for us, and we would have such a good time talking.

By Our Love *149*

Noor watched over us like a mother hen. He took us to the bazaar, to the fort on the hill, to his mosque, and to the homes of friends. He made sure that we only purchased cloth or carvings from reputable dealers. His wife, mother, sister, and three brothers, who did not know English, treated us like members of the family. Noor's mother had us try on her big silver earrings, and his wife brought out her brocaded wedding outfit for us to dress up in just for fun. Their smiles and laughter, kindness, and compassion warmed our hearts even more than the crockery-lined wicker basket of hot coals.

Noor and his family were such a blessing to us during our stay in Kashmir. Now, whenever I hear that familiar refrain, "They'll know we are Christians by our love,"[19] I think of them and pray that I as a Christian will show as much love to others as that gentle Muslim family showed to me.

For Reflection

1. Describe a time when you received an unexpected act of kindness from someone of a different religion or ethnic group.
2. Should we naturally expect Christians to show more love than non-Christians? Why or why not?
3. Do others know that you are Christian by your love?

May we reflect your love by giving selflessly for the benefit of others.

One of Them

"My lord," he said, "if it pleases you, stop here for a while. Rest in the shade of this tree while water is brought to wash your feet. And since you've honored your servant with this visit, let me prepare some food to refresh you before you continue on your journey."

—Genesis 18:3-5

"AND HERE ARE twelve bars of your favorite goat cheese!" the mother of the college president exclaimed as she hugged me and waved good-bye. "Remember to soak the cheese in water before you eat it." I was so choked up that I could hardly say a word, for I had come as a stranger but was leaving as a friend.

Sent to this small Palestinian village several weeks earlier as a library consultant for Birzeit College (now Birzeit University in Ramallah), I had been welcomed by the president with open arms and a very strong cup of coffee. For a month the librarian and another teacher had shared their little room at one end of the men's dormitory with me. They had included me in all of their activities—meals in the cafeteria, daily devotions, animated late-night discussions about the Israeli-Palestinian conflict, and walks through the stone village to buy snacks or visit a sick friend.

The president's family had invited me for dinner several times too—delightful informal occasions where I had been treated like a member of the family. The president's wife had even shown me how to put on eye makeup like the Palestinian women do.

As I stepped into the president's car to return to Jerusalem, I realized that this had not been just another overseas mission assignment. Rather, it had been a lesson in hospitality. These Christian Palestinians had showered me with love and the gift of companionship. I had arrived alone as a stranger but had been accepted as one of them in Christ. I felt more blessed than I deserved and still had twelve bars of goat cheese to enjoy. Who could ever ask for more?

For Reflection

1. Do you frequently open up your home to guests? What do you do to make them feel comfortable?
2. Have you ever had hospitality extended to you as an outsider? What were the circumstances, and how did you feel at the time?
3. What could you do to show more Christian hospitality to others?

Teach us the art of hospitality, that no one might feel a stranger among us.

Across Cultural Divides

Brothers and sisters, we urge you to warn those who are lazy. Encourage those who are timid. Take tender care of those who are weak. Be patient with everyone.
—1 Thessalonians 5:14

"DIFFERENT STROKES FOR different folks" might be the way Paul would put it if he lived in today's world. When we are dealing with people, there are certainly no "one size fits all" solutions. Each situation needs to be assessed individually if we are to respond appropriately, particularly when we are dealing with people of other cultures who are requesting our help.

When we do not assess the situation carefully, we tend to see it from our own point of view—from the needs of the donor rather than from the needs of the recipient. When people from around the world came to the aid of 2004 Southeast Asia tsunami survivors, for example, some sent funds to reliable relief organizations, but many others sent woolen jackets, bathing suits, and whatever they wanted to weed out of their closets. One New York report indicated that over 1,000 pairs of shoes had been donated for the Aceh survivors. Many of the shoes, however, were unsuitable for use in the tropics or too large for Indonesian feet.

When we do not assess the situation carefully, we also assume that people of another culture see things as we do. We offer solutions that would be appropriate in our own cultural setting but not in theirs. Take, for example, how the Indonesian government, based in Java, tried to provide basic services for the people of East Timor before the nation of Timor Leste was formed in 2001. How difficult and expensive it was for the Indonesian government to make basic health and education services available when the East Timorese lived in farmhouses scattered all over the mountainous terrain! How much easier it would be if these residents lived together in a community like Indonesians did on the island of Java. With good intentions, then, government officials built an urban housing settlement in the valley for the East Timorese, with rows of houses close together. They had failed to recognize, though, that people's need for space differs from culture to culture. The East Timorese refused to stay in the new settlement, not because they were unappreciative of the government's efforts, but because they did not feel comfortable living close together in a housing complex. It simply did not suit their farming-based lifestyle.

When we do not assess the situation carefully, we give what we ourselves would value or prefer rather than what the other person would need or find appealing. We experienced this when we moved into a university faculty housing complex on Java for the first time. A neighbor who hailed from the island of Sumba dropped over to welcome us to the neighborhood. He presented me with a covered dish that would have been highly valued in his own culture. It certainly wasn't in mine. When I lifted the lid, what did I find but generous portions of grilled dog!

Do we assess each situation carefully and really understand people's problems before we respond to them? Do we show sensitivity as we reach across cultural divides to meet the needs of others?

For Reflection

1. What message does 1 Thessalonians 5:14 offer us as we relate to other people?
2. What problems have you encountered when trying to reach across the cultural divide to meet the needs of others?
3. What can we do to learn about the culture and lifestyle of people in other areas before we attempt to meet their needs?

As we extend Christian compassion across cultural divides, may we assess each situation carefully and give with a sensitive heart.

Let Me Help!

> If one part suffers, all the parts suffer with it, and if one part is honored, all the parts are glad.
> —1 Corinthians 12:26

"I'VE BEEN A Christian psychotherapist for twenty years, and Indonesia needs my skills right now," the email stated. "Tell me how I can volunteer my help."

When the 2004 tsunami devastated Aceh, we received many such emails from people around the world who felt the suffering and longed to be an active part of the solution. Their hearts were in the right place. They did not seem to realize, however, that global disaster relief work requires professionals with technical skills and prior experience in disaster relief work. Unfortunately, too, well-meaning foreign volunteers need sponsorship in order to get a visa. They also tend to get in the way, taking up food, accommodations, and supplies needed by residents and local professional workers.

Even though the psychotherapist who contacted us had professional skills and experience, he did not have a working knowledge of the local language, had never worked in a developing country before, and was not familiar with the culture of the area. Would the methods he used in an individual-oriented culture like the United States even be suitable or effective in an Asian group-oriented culture? What could he accomplish?

Volunteers can be such a blessing in a domestic disaster. This is usually not the case in a global disaster, however, where it is far more cost-effective and sustainable to hire qualified survivors. Then too, reliable international relief agencies usually have established a strong presence in the area long before a disaster strikes and are more adept than volunteers at assessing survivor needs and meeting those needs.

When an international disaster strikes, instead of volunteering, consider sending money to dependable aid organizations. Monetary gifts will help agencies such as Action by Churches Together and Church World Service provide a reliable, coordinated relief effort for those who are suffering.

For Reflection

1. Have you ever worked as a volunteer in a disaster relief effort? What did you learn from the experience?
2. What disaster relief efforts have you supported in other ways?
3. Why would it be better to send donations to relief agencies instead of to local churches in the disaster area?

Teach us to share the burdens of those who suffer, Lord, in ways that honor them and please you most.

Chapter 10

A Matter of Perception

The eye sees only what the mind is prepared to comprehend.[20]

—Robertson Davies

Looking Beneath the Surface

⸺∰⸺

Look beneath the surface so you can judge correctly.
—John 7:24

WHAT DO YOU usually eat for breakfast? In Java we often eat fried rice, sticky rice, or rice served up with vegetables or chicken soup. A Canadian visitor staying with our Indonesian neighbor once complained to me about this.

"The only problem I have staying with your neighbor is having breakfast," she said. "I can't stand eating rice for breakfast. I'd rather eat snakes than eat rice! I'll have to teach her how to make a proper breakfast."

It doesn't take long for those of us who travel or live in another culture to discover that we don't all eat alike. Few Indonesians like blue cheese or know how to eat corn flakes. My Javanese neighbors serve sweet cakes as an appetizer instead of a dessert. The covered dish our friends from Manado always love to bring to church potlucks is curried dog.

No, we don't all eat alike. Neither do we look alike, dress alike, think alike, or act alike. And why should we? God created us to be different. If God accepts us and loves us despite our differences, shouldn't we also learn to accept and love others just as they are without trying to impose our standards on them?

When we look beneath the surface and see one another as God does, we begin to honor and cherish our differences. In the family of God, no one is a stranger at the table.

For Reflection

1. Has anyone ever judged you negatively and tried to make you what you are not? How did it make you feel at the time?
2. Have you ever felt that you were so different from others that you didn't belong? What caused you to feel that way?
3. Describe someone in your family who is very different from you but whom you have come to appreciate.

Help us, Creator God, to recognize and celebrate our differences, and, in so doing, to treat others as we expect others to treat us.

Different Perspectives

"My thoughts are nothing like your thoughts," says the Lord, "and my ways are far beyond anything you could imagine."
—Isaiah 55:8

WHEN WE LIVE in another culture, we soon realize that people see things differently than we do and operate by different rules and principles. It takes a long time to really understand the underlying assumptions and values people have—sometimes even years.

I had lived in Central Java for nearly two decades when our university decided to expand its library. As library director, I was consulting with a Javanese colleague about the layout of our new building. He kept insisting that the reference room was to the right of the main entrance; I knew for a fact that it was to the left. Showing him the blueprint, I pointed to the reference room on the left.

"Like I said," he insisted, "the reference room is to the right of the entrance."

It was only then that I realized that he was looking at the blueprint as though he were standing inside of the building facing the entrance instead of outside of it looking in, as I was. We had both taken for granted that we were operating under the same cultural assumptions.

On another level, don't we often tend to do the same thing with God? We view the situation from our own perspective and assume that God is not only seeing it as we are but is operating under the same principles as we are too. We forget that God's ways are not like our ways and then wonder why God has not answered our prayers in the way we expect. Should we not be trying to fit ourselves into his plans instead of expecting him to fit himself into ours?

For Reflection

1. Have you and a friend or colleague ever looked at the same thing and discovered that you were seeing it differently?
2. Think of a time when you realized God's plans were different than your own. What made you realize it, and what did you do?
3. How can we be sure that we are fitting into God's plans?

Open our eyes to see that your perspective on our situation is often different from our own and to acknowledge that your way is always best.

Friendship Is the Best Policy

> How wonderful to be wise, to analyze and interpret things.
> —Ecclesiastes 8:1

SURELY MY STUDENTS knew better than to try to cheat, yet there sat a student boldly copying answers from a friend's paper during the final exam I was giving at our Christian university in Central Java. When I called them into my office afterwards, the first student readily admitted that she had copied from her friend's answer sheet.

"But why did you let her do that?" I asked the second.

Shaking her head as though I were daft, she exclaimed, "There's nothing wrong with helping a friend, is there?"

In her cultural upbringing, maintaining good relationships with those she knew and loved was mandatory. Nothing was more important than helping a friend, even if it meant breaking the rules to do so. After all, rules are made to be broken. I had been culturally conditioned to see it differently. To me, nothing trumped honesty, fairness, and following the rules. Like most people, I had not only assumed that my own cultural values were best but that they were universal.

Those who work in cultural contexts other than their own continually confront these kinds of situations. Granted, we may not agree with the underlying assumptions and values of another culture, but at least we need to be aware of them and try to understand them, for it is only when we understand them that we can be effective in our work.

For Reflection

1. If you were the teacher, what would you have said to the student who saw nothing wrong with helping a friend?
2. Describe a value in another culture or tradition that you have trouble accepting.
3. What can we do to discover, analyze, and interpret the underlying values of people in another culture?

Give us the sensitivity, wisdom, and compassion we need to be effective in our work wherever we may serve in God's world.

But Aren't the Jews Christian?

> Look, I am sending you out as sheep among wolves. So be as shrewd as snakes and harmless as doves.
> —Matthew 10:16

FIVE YEARS AFTER the 1967 War, when Israel had defeated Egypt, Jordan, and Syria, I was sent to the West Bank town of Birzeit to serve as a short-term library consultant at a Palestinian Christian college.

Chatting with the college president in his office that first week, I asked, "Do you have any Jews enrolled here?"

Turning to me with a wry smile he replied, "Well, I tell you, Rosie, I've never had the privilege of turning one down."

I had asked a stupid question, indeed, but how was I to know? I had grown up with American Jewish schoolmates and only knew what I had read in frequently unbalanced newspaper reports. Once among the Palestinian Christians, I soon learned that the Israeli-Palestinian problem was not just a political conflict but a religious one as well. For my Palestinian Christian friends, Israeli Jews were the enemy.

Fast forward to Java, Indonesia, thirty-seven years later. "Shalom!" the pastor exclaimed from the pulpit at our small church in Salatiga.

"Shalom!" the congregation responded in turn.

Our American guest, who had not graced the pew of a church for years, was shocked. After all, she reasoned, "shalom" was a Hebrew word used by the American Jewish community. "Don't they know that's Jewish, not Christian?" she asked as we sat around the dining room table after supper.

Our Timorese cousin was baffled by her question. "But the Jews are Christian, aren't they?" he asked. "After all, we have both the Old Testament and the New Testament in our Christian Bible, don't we?"

Well, how could we expect him to know any more about Jews and Christians than I did when I first visited the Palestinian Territories, I reasoned. After all, Indonesia only recognized six religions, and Judaism was not one of them.

For Reflection

1. How would you respond to someone who insisted that the Jews are Christian?
2. What challenges are Palestinian and Arab Christians currently facing? What, if anything, are our churches doing to support their cause?
3. What can we do to ensure that the news we receive about today's world is as balanced and impartial as possible?

Help us to become shrewd enough to see beyond our own misconceptions for the sake of truth and justice.

Different Cultural Lenses

Love each other with genuine affection, and take delight in honoring each other.
—Romans 12:10

CHRISTIAN VALUES ARE the same the world over, but how these values are expressed often differs from culture to culture. Take compassion, for instance. Christians everywhere know the meaning of compassion. How we show our compassion, however, may differ because of cultural values that come into play.

Last year, for example, we went to the hospital to visit an elderly member of our congregation. As we entered the small hospital room, the patient's husband held her hand affectionately and told us, "We thought the cancer had returned, but the diagnostic tests show that everything is clear! My wife will be going home tomorrow." How relieved we were to hear this good news.

A month later, however, word came that our friend's wife had died of cancer. We were shocked and immediately questioned the validity of the diagnostic tests. Only then did the husband admit to us that the tests had diagnosed her cancer accurately. He explained that he had kept it a secret from his wife so that she wouldn't worry.

The wife, it turns out, had been equally compassionate toward her spouse. Even though her husband knew that she was failing fast, her death had come as a surprise to him that morning—but not to their daughter. The wife had told their daughter that she didn't expect to live through the night but had warned her not to tell her father because she didn't want him to worry or lose sleep.

As an American, I found this confusing. To me, sharing their pain together openly and honestly would have been the most compassionate thing to do. To them and many other Indonesians like them, protecting others from the truth is often the most compassionate thing they feel they can do.

For Reflection

1. What problems arise when we see the world through our own cultural lenses?
2. How do cultural differences impact the work of the church internationally?
3. What problems are apt to arise when churches send volunteer missionaries overseas on short-term assignments with little or no cross-cultural training?

Help us not to fear our differences but to try to understand them and honor them, recognizing that diversity can enrich us and strengthen our relationships.

We and They

But if I don't understand a language, I will be a foreigner to someone who speaks it, and the one who speaks it will be a foreigner to me.
—1 Corinthians 14:11

All the people like us are We, And everyone else is They.[21]
—Rudyard Kipling

WHEN OUR ELCA missionaries from India, Nepal, Thailand, and Indonesia held a retreat at the tip of South India, two buses drove us from Chennai to Mahabalipuram. Daniel and I were in the second bus, which was going much slower than the first.

When we arrived in Mahabalipuram, our bus driver looked confused because he didn't know where the first bus had gone. Only the first driver knew how to get to our retreat center. Some of the missionaries also knew the way and tried to give our driver directions. When their explanations fell on deaf ears, we assumed he didn't know English. Instead of responding, he got off the bus and tried to ask people along the road where the other bus had gone.

Finally Daniel, a Timorese who is often mistaken for an Indian, got off the bus and started talking to the driver. As the two continued their discussion, a missionary sitting in back of me exclaimed, "I didn't know Daniel spoke Tamil!" Well, neither did I. He and the driver were carrying on a lively conversation, though, and the driver was obviously satisfied with the directions Daniel was giving. The two of them finally climbed back on the bus, and off we drove to the retreat center.

"Why did he follow your directions but not ours?" everyone asked.

As it turned out, the driver knew English but had felt much more comfortable speaking with Daniel instead of all those "foreigners."

So many times we define ourselves by our differences—differences which create communication barriers and alienate us from other people. What would happen if we concentrated on the similarities that unite us instead?

For Reflection

1. Have physical or cultural differences with other people ever created a communication barrier for you or made you feel uncomfortable?
2. Who are the "We"s and the "They"s in your life?
3. What practical things can you do to make the "They"s of your life become "Us"?

Help us to focus on the similarities that unite us instead of the differences that divide us.

Chapter 11
Promoting Harmony

> If we cannot end our differences, at least we can help make the world safe for diversity.[22]
> —John F. Kennedy

High Maintenance

How wonderful and pleasant it is when brothers live together in harmony!
—Psalm 133:1

HARMONY WITHIN A family is precious. In an extended family like ours, harmonious relations are essential to the well-being of the whole, and staying connected is not something to be taken for granted. Like houses in the tropics, these relationships require careful maintenance, sometimes in ways that are not always obvious to those of us who have been raised in another culture.

When my husband's younger brother married a girl from a different island, our Timorese extended family was expected to pay thirty head of water

buffalo to the bride's family as a dowry. We had saved for this and were ready. As our two families met to discuss the transaction, though, I was surprised to hear my husband say, "We can only pay for twenty at this time." The other family considered this and then agreed that we could pay the dowry off in installments.

It did not make any sense to me at all. "Why did you delay?" I asked my husband when the family meeting had ended. "Why not pay off the full amount and be done with it?"

"Well, if I had done that," he replied, "the transaction would be finished. This way we still owe them something and have a reason to continue the relationship between us. It's a way of staying connected with our new in-laws."

Harmonious relationships are important for Christians. Sustaining good relations within our families, neighborhoods, and churches is not always easy, but as members of the family of God, we know that we have been designed to relate to others as God relates to us. When we are attentive and careful, such relationships can be achieved, maintained, and enjoyed to the benefit of all.

For Reflection

1. Which relationships are most important to you in your own family?
2. What are some rules for being a good in-law in your culture?
3. Which relationships within your own family seem strained? What can you do to strengthen those relationships?

Creator God, help us to be aware of the importance of our relationships and the wisdom to do what it takes to maintain them and strengthen them.

Winning the Battle

Control your temper, for anger labels you a fool.
—Ecclesiastes 7:9

WITH ARMS CROSSED defiantly, Bambang slouched in his chair and glared at me. All of the other Indonesian students in my English class at Satya Wacana Christian University were attentive and participating actively, but Bambang sat there as cold as a rock, making snide remarks.

If you have ever been a teacher or taught a Sunday school class, you know the feeling. What do you do with students like that—jerk them to attention and embarrass them in front of their friends? Feeling angry and irritated, I was tempted, but I knew harsh words would probably only make things worse, especially in a culture like Java, where conflict is avoided at all costs.

Whether in church, school, or the boardroom, controlling our tempers can bring win-win solutions, for people like Bambang can sometimes surprise us. Like geodes, they look pretty rough on the outside but often harbor surprises on the inside. By forcing ourselves to remain patient and gentle, we can unexpectedly bring out the best they have to offer, as I discovered in that class as the semester progressed.

One day when I was having trouble with the projector, a student suddenly appeared at my side and started checking the program on my laptop for me. I was startled, for it was Bambang. Once he had things running, he suggested that he sit in my chair and show the power point slides as I talked. That certainly made my job easier. After class he smiled and said, "Just let me know if you need help. I'm good at this." For the rest of the semester, Bambang set up the equipment for me and ran the projector. I really don't know what I would have done without him.

As we journey down the road of life, we meet up with a lot of disgruntled people who rub us the wrong way. When we fight fire with fire, tempers flare and we both get burned. Gandhi put it well when he said, "To lose patience is to lose the battle."[23] When we aim for harmony through patience, tolerance, and goodwill, we not only win the battle but bring out the best in others and ourselves as well.

For Reflection

1. Who in your home, church, or place of work is most skillful at keeping the peace and bringing out the best in others?
2. How do you handle people who continually disagree with you?
3. What contentious situations do you face in your church or place of work? What steps could you take to promote harmony instead?

Help us, oh Lord, to seek harmony and to pursue those things which make for peace.

The Test of Tolerance

～❀◎

> But the Holy Spirit produces this kind of fruit in our lives: love, joy, peace, patience, kindness, goodness, faithfulness, gentleness, and self-control. There is no law against these things!
>
> —Galatians 5:22-23

INDONESIA HAS MORE Muslims than all of the nations of the Middle East put together. Only eight or nine percent of the population is Christian, and less than three percent of the population is enrolled in colleges and universities.

The percentage of Muslims at Satya Wacana Christian University has grown from fifteen percent in 1978 to forty percent today. Why would Muslims want to attend a Christian university when there are hundreds of public and Muslim universities to choose from? Ask them and they will tell you that it is not only our academic excellence that draws them but our way of life—our respect for differences of opinion, nondiscriminatory services, and caring nature.

When I receive a framed cross from one of my Muslim students at graduation and a Muslim alumnus insists on putting "Ph.D., Satya Wacana Christian University" at the end of every newspaper column he writes, we know the extremists' ravine of hate is being bridged. We are succeeding because our university's leaders insist it is not how big we are that matters but how we present ourselves as Christians.

Christians are in the minority in Indonesia, and that takes courage. What happens when the minority becomes the majority, such as Christians do when they enroll at a Christian university in Indonesia? What then? As Ralph W. Sockman put it, "The test of courage comes when we are in the minority. The test of tolerance comes when we are in the majority."[24]

For Reflection

1. Is there a limit to Christian tolerance? When is it appropriate to be tolerant, and when is it not?
2. What intolerance toward minority religious groups have you witnessed in the place where you reside?
3. In what specific ways can we encourage our children and neighbors to be more understanding and tolerant?

Whether we are the minority or the majority, may the way we present ourselves as Christians be worthy of the one who enables us to have life and to have it more abundantly.

To Know Them Is To Love Them

No one has ever seen God. But if we love each other, God lives in us, and his love is brought to full expression in us.
—1 John 4:12

"*MINAL' AIDIN WALFAIZIN!*" the ladies of our English conversation group exclaimed, greeting each other with the traditional Arabic expression of congratulations for successfully completing the fast. They were not gathered for an English lesson from me this time but to celebrate the Muslim festival of Idul Fitri together.

Idul Fitri is the most important festival in Islam, marking the end of the fasting month. Each year, the group meets at a Muslim's home to listen to the Muslim members of the group present speeches in English on the custom of fasting during Ramadan and their religious values and convictions. This formal part of the program is always followed by a meal together with traditional Idul Fitri delicacies.

At Christmastime the roles are reversed. In December, we meet at the home of a Christian, and the Christians put on a program for the Muslims of the group. The program often consists of a worship service complete with sermon, carols, and prayers. Last year they even invited a keyboard musician from a neighboring town to play for the worship service and the meal which followed.

In a nation where nearly ninety percent of the population is Muslim, I am amazed at how the desire to learn English has so unassumingly brought these Muslim and Christian women together and broken down the barriers between them. Their desire to learn has not only improved their English but encouraged mutual understanding and respect as well.

How much more effective our witness is when we show genuine love for one another. Is it not through listening, learning, serving, and sharing together that Christians best testify to the love experienced in Christ?

For Reflection

1. What do you think would happen if the Muslims or Christians of this group crossed the line and openly tried to convert members of the other faith?
2. What groups have you belonged to which have encouraged you to share your religious convictions with people of another faith?

3. What other opportunities have you found to give witness to your faith through love, concern, care, and service for non-Christians?

Help us to testify to the love of Christ by showing interest and concern for those whose beliefs may be very different from our own.

Ulterior Motives

> But that doesn't matter. Whether their motives are false or genuine, the message about Christ is being preached either way, so I rejoice. And I will continue to rejoice.
> —Philippians 1:15

WHEN WE LIVED in Australia, our church put on a free Christmas lunch for anyone who needed a place to go on Christmas Day. It was a chance to bring joy to the elderly, to those who lived alone, and to international students. Our community enthusiastically supported the event.

The Manahan Javanese Christian Church in Surakarta, Central Java, does something similar—not for the community at large at Christmas, but for Muslims who are fasting during the holy month of Ramadan. For more than a dozen years now, members of the congregation have set up tables and chairs in front of the church and down the street to serve the evening meal to Muslims who are breaking the fast. Their efforts are especially aimed at day laborers and pedicab drivers who work long hours for little pay and have a hard time making ends meet. The meals are not free but very inexpensive and nourishing.

Even though disadvantaged Muslims benefit from breaking the fast at this church, not everyone is happy about it. Last year a number of Islamic groups sent letters of complaint to the police, questioning the motives of the church. Were they really trying to help the Muslims, or were they trying to convert them?

Since evangelism is not allowed in Indonesia, the police took the complaints seriously and banned the church from providing meals to Muslims during Ramadan. The pastor of the church insisted that their motives were innocent and that the meals were an effort to promote religious tolerance and assist the poorer members of society as they prepared for the Idul Fitri holidays. Several local Muslims also commended the church for promoting religious tolerance in such an innovative way. The police finally concluded that no religious activities were taking place during the event and lifted the ban the following week.

For Reflection

1. Would your community support your church's efforts if it served free meals to those who had no place to go on Christmas Day?
2. How would your community feel if Muslims, Buddhists, or Hindus hosted the event? Would you be suspicious of their motives?
3. Is it ethical for Christians to attempt to evangelize or smuggle Bibles into a country that bans proselytism? Do the ends justify the means?

May our motives be pure as we witness to God's love and purpose through Jesus Christ.

Breaking Down
the Stereotypes

For you will be treated as you treat others. The standard you use in judging is the standard by which you will be judged.
—Matthew 7:2

SPRAWLED OUT ON the floor, Pri called out, "Try moving that string of lights a little higher, Vera! Here, let me help!" It was early December, and my sister-in-law was up on a ladder decorating the gorgeous tree that graced our living room.

Pri, an electrician by trade, was a frequent visitor to our house. It warmed our hearts to watch him adjust the lights and exclaim over the magnificent tree. You see, in Indonesia only Christians celebrate Christmas. Pri is a Muslim.

"What—a Muslim?" our American visitor asked. "Are you sure? He doesn't sound like someone who hates nonbelievers or puts women down."

Obviously she had a lot to learn, but then so did I. How is it that an Indonesian Muslim knows so much about decorating a Christmas tree, I wondered.

Curious, I asked Pri that day. He explained that he had attended a Christian vocational school, and from that experience he had learned a lot about the way Christians live.

When Muslims attend Christian schools and universities, they may not convert because of the experience, but they come away with a deeper appreciation of our religion and way of life. As Muslims and Christians live together as neighbors or serve together in the workplace, they break down the stereotypes and become less judgmental, more discerning, and more tolerant of each other.

For Reflection

1. What stereotypes or fixed impressions do you or other people in your community have of Muslims? Hindus? Buddhists? Jews?
2. Why are stereotypes of other people and other religions so harmful?
3. In an effort to promote harmony, how should we respond when we hear negative stereotypes leveled at a person of another religion or ethnic group?

Help us, oh Lord, to break down harmful and degrading stereotypes that prevent us from seeing the good in other people.

Bridging the Ravine

Such love has no fear, because perfect love expels all fear.
—1 John 4:18

WHEN MY HUSBAND was studying for his PhD in Australia, he struck up a warm friendship with three other international students in the same program. One day, we invited the three of them over to our house for dinner.

"We'd love to come!" they exclaimed enthusiastically. Then, with a bit of hesitancy, they asked, "But what are you planning to serve?"

"Something you will like," I said. "Beef curry."

"Wonderful!" they chimed and then asked, "Would you mind if we bought the meat for you?"

Normally a question like that would have surprised me, but this time it didn't. You see, our three friends were Pakistani Muslims, and Muslims, like Jews, only eat meat that has been slaughtered in a prescribed way. So, they bought the meat from their mosque, and we did the cooking. Together we enjoyed a delightful evening of fellowship.

I was reminded of that occasion recently when once again we invited students over to the house. Our guests were students in one of Daniel's graduate courses at Satya Wacana Christian University in Central Java. It was the last class of the semester, and we would end it with dinner together.

As they came in the door, several asked if they could pray before the class began. By this they did not mean having a two-minute prayer together around the circle; twenty-one of the twenty-five, after all, were Muslims who prayed five times a day and needed to pray according to Islamic teachings. Like Jews, Muslims emphasize ritual purity. For cleansing themselves before *salat* (ritual prayer), they used our two downstairs bathrooms. Because we had moved the front room furniture into the living room for the class, there was plenty of floor space in that room and the guest bedroom to spread out large, woven Timorese cloths as prayer rugs.

After prayers, the class gathered in the living room for a warm and animated evaluation of what they had learned in their semester-long course on human resource management training.

190 Light for the Journey

For the dinner that followed, they had brought several tempting dishes to add to what we had already cooked, and we enjoyed a delectable meal together. But that's not all. After the meal, they asked us to gather together in the living room once more. They read poems they had written for Professor Daniel and gave speeches expressing their delight in his teaching. Their eyes were filled with love as they presented us with gifts.

Where is this ravine of hate that extremists like Abu Bakar Ba'asyir proclaim? Indeed there are terrorists, and the problem has grown worse since 9/11, but what good does it do to ignorantly assume that all Muslims are terrorists or even that ten percent of them are? The extremists' ravine of hate grows wider when we allow ourselves to think the way extremists do. The ravine of hate becomes more difficult to bridge when we propagate fear instead of love.

For Reflection

1. When we promote fear, we promote hate. Who do you fear, and what are you doing to dispel those fears?
2. Indonesians often say that we have to know a person before we can love him. How does getting to know people of other cultures, religions, and traditions help to break down the walls of fear and distrust?
3. Mark Twain once warned, "If you think knowledge is dangerous, try ignorance."[25] What role has ignorance played in creating a more dangerous society for us all since 9/11?

God of love, help us to remember that love casts out fear and that as followers of Christ, we are to show acts of love and kindness to all whom you have created.

Finding Common Ground

> But anyone who hates another brother or sister is still living and walking in darkness. Such a person does not know the way to go, having been blinded by the darkness.
> —1 John 2:11

CAN A DESTRUCTIVE power be harnessed for a constructive purpose? Conflicts between Muslims and Christians have killed thousands of Indonesians since 2000. As each retaliates against the other, both sides have been blinded by the darkness. Fortunately, the increasing cycle of violence has not prevented religious groups from trying to bring opposing groups together to work for the common good.

One way to do that is to establish interfaith centers or to sponsor religious dialogs to promote peace. Another way, which can involve people at the grassroots level, is to bring opposing groups together to solve a common problem.

Several years ago when avian flu began sweeping across the Indonesian archipelago, Indonesia's largest Islamic organization, Nahdlatul Ulama (NU), decided to hold a conference to develop a national awareness program about avian flu. Instead of doing it by themselves, they asked our Christian university to join them and sponsor it together. Muslim and Christian health officials, veterinarians, and academics came together to study the situation. They worked tirelessly and came up with preventive measures that were implemented throughout the nation to ward off a national disaster. To convince people that chicken was safe to eat, they ended their conference by eating chicken together.

We walk in the darkness when we use violence to defend our beliefs and seek revenge for wrongs. We walk in the light when we work to develop mutual trust and cooperation instead. To enhance mutual understanding, we can educate ourselves about the other faith tradition and bring theologians and religious leaders together for dialog. It's even better when we use indirect approaches as well. When we bring opposing groups together to solve a common problem, we not only solve the problem together but promote peace and harmony in the process.

For Reflection

1. Have you ever participated in interfaith dialogs or activities? If so, how were you affected by the experience?
2. What problems does your community face that could be solved by bringing people of different faiths together to work for a common cause?
3. What lessons have you learned from relating to people of other faiths?

May we never let our religious differences keep us from caring personally about each other and finding common ground for the sake of all.

Endnotes

1. Edward K. Rowell, ed., *Quotes and Idea Starters for Preaching and Teaching from Leadership Journal* (Grand Rapids: Baker Books,1996), 60.
2. Evelyn Underhill. Beliefnet.com Quote library, http://www.beliefnet.com/Quotes/Christian/E/Evelyn-Underhill/If-God-Were-Small-Enough-To-Be-Understood-He-Woul.aspx (accessed June 25, 2011).
3. Iwan Satyanegara Kamah, "Orang tidurpun dibela Gus Dur", GUSDURian, http://gusdurian.net/news/2011/05/24/52/orang_tidurpun_dibela_gus_dur.html, May 24, 2011 (accessed June 26, 2011).
4. David G. Myers, *Psychology*. 5th ed. (New York: Worth Publishers, 1998), 192.
5. Ibid.
6 Peter Gomes, *Sermons: Biblical Wisdom for Daily Living* (New York: Avon Books, 1998), 125.
7. Dwight L. Moody. Tentmaker, Quotes on Grace. http://www.tentmaker.org/Quotes/grace_quotes.html (accessed June 25, 2011).

8. Edith Wharton. The Quote Garden, Quotations about Light. http://www.quotegarden.com/light.html (accessed June 25, 2011).
9. G.K. Chesterton. The Quote Garden, Quotations about Perspective. http://www.quotegarden.com/perspective.html (accessed June 24, 2011).
10. M. Kathleen Casey. The Quote Garden, Quotations about Adversity. http://www.quotegarden.com/adversity.html (accessed June 15, 2011).
11. Greg Fealy, "Hating Americans: Jemaah Islamiyah and the Bali Bombings," IIAS Newsletter no.31 (July 2003): 3. http://www.iias.nl/nl/31/IIAS_NL31_0304.pdf (accessed June 24, 2011).
12. Tekmito Adegemo. Laboring in the Lord. http://laboringinthelord.com/2011/04/03/sunday-quotes-04-03-11/ (accessed June 26, 2011).
13. Philip Gulley. The Quote Garden, Quotations about Worrying. http://www.quotegarden.com/worry.html (accessed June 24, 2011).
14. Adegemo, Laboring in the Lord.
15. Voltaire. Great-Quotes.com, Gledhill Enterprises, 2011. http://www.great-quotes.com/quote/1377833, (accessed June 25, 2011).
16. Kent Nerburn, *Make Me An Instrument of Your Peace: Living in the Spirit of the Prayer of Saint Francis.* (San Francisco: HarperSanFrancisco, 1999).
17. Virginia Satir, *Making Contact.* (Berkeley: Celestial Arts,1976), n.p., under "You Own All the Tools You Need".
18. Paul Tillich. Great-Quotes.com, Gledhill Enterprises, 2011. http://www.great-quotes.com/quote/318, (accessed June 25, 2011).
19. A well-known phrase from a Christian hymn written in 1968 by then-Catholic priest Peter R. Scholtes.

20. Robertson Davies. Great-Quotes.com, Gledhill Enterprises, 2011. http://www.great-quotes.com/quote/642835, (accessed June 25, 2011).
21. Rudyard Kipling. The Kipling Society. http://www.kipling.org.uk/poems_wethey.htm, (accessed June 27, 2011).
22. M. Scott Peck, ed., *Abounding Grace; an Anthology of Wisdom*. (Kansas City, Missouri: Andrews McMeel Publishing, 2000), 325.
23. Ibid, 154.
24. Ralph W. Sockman, The Quote Garden, Quotations about Prejudice. http://www.quotegarden.com/prejudice.html (accessed June 25, 2011).
25. Mark Twain. Great-Quotes.com, Gledhill Enterprises, 2011. http://www.great-quotes.com/quote/47878 (accessed June 25, 2011).

Scriptural Index

Genesis
1:27.................................43
18:3-5 151
32:27-28 35

Exodus
14:10.............................117

Leviticus
19:18 148
19:31................................8

Joshua
1:9.................................109

Job
2:7-10 93

Psalms
16:11...............................71
19:1.................................26
22:1.................................97
31:22.............................115
32:8-9 3
46:1-2 99
50:15...............................91
51:3...............................127
133:1.............................175

Proverbs
2:11...............................131
3:6....................................5
4:7.................................129
5:1...................................82
10:8.................................77
10:9...............................121
17:17.............................140
27:19...............................33

Ecclesiastes
2:11.................................46
7:9.................................177
8:1.................................165

Isaiah
55:8 163

Habakkuk
3:17-18 101

Matthew
6:7-8 22
7:2 186
10:16 167
17:27 13
18:5 123
20:26 86
22:28-29 28
25:35 146

Mark
4:40 113

Luke
12:6-7 37

John
7:24 161
14:27 111

Romans
11:6 59
12:10 169
12:14 95

1 Corinthians
8:9 61
12:26 157
14:11 171

2 Corinthians
3:18 39
4:8-9 104
8:12 135
12:9 80

Galatians
5:1 55
5:4 57
5:22-23 179
6:2 142

Ephesians
1:8 24

Philippians
1:15 184
1:27 84

Colossians
3:12 137
3:14 48

1 Thessalonians
3:12-13 68
5:14 154
5:16-18 20

Hebrews
5:11 65
11:1 10

James
1:19 144

1 Peter
2:9 41
3:15 74

1 John
1:9 53
2:11 192
3:1 17
3:6 125
4:12 181
4:18 188

WinePressPublishing
Great Books, Defined.

To order additional copies of this book call:
1-877-421-READ (7323)
or please visit our website at
www.WinePressbooks.com

If you enjoyed this quality custom-published book, drop by our website for more books and information.

www.winepresspublishing.com
"Your partner in custom publishing."

CPSIA information can be obtained at www.ICGtesting.com
Printed in the USA
BVOW030541161012

303104BV00001B/84/P